DESIGNING SOLUTIONS FOR YOUR BUSINESS PROBLEMS

A Structured Process for Managers and Consultants

Betty Vandenbosch

JOSSEY-BASS
A Wiley Imprint
www.josseybass.com

Published by Jossey-Bass
A Wiley Imprint
989 Market Street, San Francisco, CA 94103-1741   www.josseybass.com

Jossey-Bass books and products are available through most bookstores. To contact Jossey-Bass directly call our Customer Care Department within the U.S. at 800-956-7739, outside the U.S. at 317-572-3986 or fax 317-572-4002.

Jossey-Bass also publishes its books in a variety of electronic formats. Some content that appears in print may not be available in electronic books.

Library of Congress Cataloging-in-Publication Data

Vandenbosch, Betty, 1956–
   Designing solutions for your business problems : a structured process for managers and consultants / by Betty Vandenbosch.—1st ed.
    p. cm.—(The Jossey-Bass business & management series)
Includes bibliographical references and index.
   ISBN 0-7879-6765-3 (alk. paper)
  1. Problem solving. 2. Management. 3. Business consultants. I. Title. II. Series.
   HD30.29.V32 2003
   658.4'03—dc21

                                        2003009617

Printed in the United States of America

FIRST EDITION
HB Printing 10 9 8 7 6 5 4 3 2 1

CONTENTS

PART THREE: DESIGNING THE SOLUTION

TABLES & FIGURES

Tables

Figures

To my parents, Martin and Ann

ACKNOWLEDGMENTS

The problem-solving process described in this book has evolved from more than two decades of consulting and teaching. Its development began with my experiences as a consultant with McKinsey & Company, where I learned best practices of problem solving and consulting from the ground up. Although the approach I describe in this book is not McKinsey's process, my experiences there had a great deal to do with my understanding of what world-class problem solving entails. I owe a debt to my many McKinsey mentors and colleagues.

I am also a director of PDN Limited, a professional services advisory firm specializing in consultancy skills training and professional development. I have borrowed liberally from the PDN materials in the development of this book and thank my partners for helping me with their insights and encouragement.

My students at the Weatherhead School of Management at Case Western Reserve University have read many of the chapters for their coursework. Their comments and criticisms have contributed to refinements of the process and its supporting tools and techniques.

Although the ideas explored here have taken years to develop, I wrote most of the book while I was on sabbatical from Weatherhead. I thank Dick Boland and Fred Collopy for giving me the freedom to write it.

I also thank the many people who read drafts of the book, some long before it was worth reading. They include Zachary Coleman, Niels Dechow, Ann Hagan,

Mike Hastings, Darrell Hawkins, William Johnson, Kenneth Lay, David Maister, Al Morrison, John Savage, Paul Stork, and Ed Wilton.

I thank Jeff Darner, Tom Helfrich, and Henry Meyer at KeyCorp. They gave me a place to work when, at home, laundry and dishes seemed more enticing than writing.

Finally, I thank Laura George. She made sure all the details were taken care of and that the end product looked like a book rather than a confusing collection of ill-formatted Word and PowerPoint files.

THE AUTHOR

Betty **Vandenbosch** has over twenty years of experience in consulting and education. She develops courses and teaches graduate students, executives, and consultants in traditional classroom and workshop settings on such topics as system thinking, communication and negotiation, consulting skills and processes, project management, and the strategic use of technology.

Vandenbosch is an associate professor of information systems at the Weatherhead School of Management at Case Western Reserve University. She researches and writes about the impact of information technology on individual and organizational performance. She is also a director of PDN Limited, a professional services development firm specializing in consultancy skills training.

Earlier in her career, she spent nearly seven years as an associate, engagement manager, and senior engagement manager with McKinsey and Company in Toronto and Amsterdam. In addition to consulting with clients on strategic, organizational, and operational issues, she developed and conducted tailored training sessions and seminars for her colleagues in North America, Europe, and Asia.

She was educated at the University of Western Ontario, where she earned a B.Sc. in Computer Science and an M.B.A. and a Ph.D. in Management Information Systems.

INTRODUCTION

I recently overheard a conversation my twelve-year-old son, Martin, had with his friend Johanna while riding in the back seat of our car. In the midst of their chatter, he proudly announced, "My mom's writing a book!"

"About what?" Johanna asked.

"Management consulting."

Unimpressed, Johanna inquired, "What is *that*?"

To this, Martin confidently replied, "A management consultant is who you call when you're in a tight spot."

Leave it to Martin to sum up a multibillion dollar industry in one sentence. Martin got it partly wrong, however. This is not a book about management consulting. Rather, it's about how to get out of a tight spot.

Managers face an endless stream of ambiguous problems and opportunities that they don't have nearly enough time, resources, or process know-how to sort through and address. Although most of them are perfectly able to understand situations, solve problems, and seize opportunities, their techniques often are inefficient. Expert problem solvers, in contrast, are masters of process, and their process know-how—their ability to scope a project, conduct an analysis, develop airtight logic, and encourage creativity—is a large part of why they are expert. This is not to imply that your solutions should be of the cookie-cutter variety—quite the contrary. But if you do not have to revisit how to move forward every time you start a project, you can spend more time concentrating on the problem or opportunity itself. *Designing Solutions for Your Business Problems* provides the process know-how, which will reduce the time and resources you will need.

This book is intended for people who are concerned with improving organizations. If you are a manager who wants to benefit from a creative and disciplined approach to problem solving, a consultant hoping to hone your skills, or thinking about becoming a management consultant, *Designing Solutions for Your Business Problems* can help you.

To say that this book is about solving problems is a vast oversimplification. The idea of a problem is inherently problematic: it focuses on what is wrong. A more fruitful and considerably more enjoyable approach to problem solving is to focus on what is possible or desirable—that is, to build on what is already good. When you look at any situation, it makes sense to view it from several angles, including examining what needs fixing and what can be built on. A solution does not necessarily have to solve a problem. The best way to stop smoking, for example, is never to start in the first place. The best way to strengthen an organization may not be to solve problems and fill gaps but rather to build on the base of capabilities it already has.

Solving problems and capitalizing on opportunities is hard. Those who need help worry that the problem solvers do not have a comprehensive understanding of the organization's context; perhaps they don't understand the business, the people, the customers, the competition. They worry that the problem solvers don't have enough experience to inform their recommendations. Problem solvers worry that those whom they are helping are not sufficiently involved, that they have been asked to solve the wrong problem, that those who need help don't understand the problem-solving process, and that they lack the know-how to move ahead once the problem solver has gone on to the next project. *Designing Solutions for Your Business Problems* helps you overcome these very real concerns.

While some problem solvers would have you believe that they have unique and superior approaches, at the process level, most expert problem solvers tackle issues and design solutions in roughly the same manner. They combine the best aspects of deductive and inductive reasoning.

Deductive reasoning is the process you use when you hypothesize the solution to a problem based on your previous experience, intuition, and the data to which you already have access. In order to find out whether you're right, you develop a series of tests or collect additional data to prove or disprove your initial point of view. The scientific method is derived from deductive reasoning.

Inductive reasoning is the process you use when you collect data in an effort to understand a situation and then sift through those data to infer "the answer." Creative problem-solving techniques rely heavily on inductive processes.

There are clear trade-offs between inductive and deductive approaches. Inductive problem solving is effective for developing a solid understanding of the situation. It has the potential to lead to new insights and is also more likely to result in broader systemic solutions. However, when using an inductive approach, you can easily stray into irrelevant investigations and waste a great deal of time. You may never reach closure.

The deductive approach is always efficient. You are much less likely to collect data you don't need, and you will usually arrive at a solution quickly. The downfall of the deductive approach is that outcomes may be self-fulfilling, and you may miss new insights.

Inductive and deductive problem solving both have strong proponents. Some people shy away from the concept of developing a hypothesis and testing it. They disparage planning in favor of celebrating emergence and muddling through and focus on the artistic and emotional aspects of human thought. They believe that deductive problem solving is inherently narrow and rigid. Other people focus exclusively on the most efficient approach. They don't want to waste time exploring options or considering implications; they just want to solve the problem as quickly as possible. Neither extreme position is tenable. An integration of inductive and deductive thinking, of ideas and analysis, and of emotion and cognition will usually result in superior performance. The process set out in this book integrates inductive and deductive thinking, ideas and analysis, and emotion and cognition. It enables you to address organizational problems and opportunities efficiently and creatively.

Designing Solutions for Your Business Problems describes the balance that is the key to success in problem solving: between speed and thoroughness, between creativity and practicality, between low cost and high quality. It explains how to achieve that balance: clarify intentions, reduce the time required for data collection, increase the validity of conclusions and decisions, and communicate more effectively.

The process is based on the premise that good solutions are designed; they aren't analyzed into existence, and they don't emerge on their own. By first developing a solid understanding of the organizational situation into which the solution must fit and keeping that understanding current throughout the problem-solving process, you ensure that the solution will work in the context of the organization in which it will be implemented. By making your logic transparent, you open your potential conclusions and solutions to legitimate debate based on facts and capabilities rather than intuition and politics. By considering and developing options rather than just presuming that a first hunch is the answer, you design the best possible solution.

Designing Solutions for Your Business Problems describes a rigorous, detailed, and very human process for solving unstructured business problems and responding to opportunities in a way that people can understand and organizations can implement. It will provide you with a set of tools and techniques to address the situations you face in a logical and coherent way.

The Results

Louis Gerstner's early and decisive actions as CEO of IBM demonstrate the power of the *Designing Solutions for Your Business Problems* approach.[1] Gerstner started his tenure in 1993 by visiting clients and employees out in the field and reading "thousands of pages of strategic documents" to enable him to understand the situation IBM was facing. Within a month, he developed a hypothesis about the wisdom of splitting the company into a federation of thirteen organizations, a move originally recommended by his predecessor, John Akers. The prevailing theory was that "as an integrated company IBM was not quick and nimble." Gerstner, a former IBM customer himself at American Express and Nabisco, hypothesized that customers might not be drawn to a federation as a model for IBM because the company was unique in its ability to help them solve complex technology problems across hardware platforms and software applications, as well as around the globe.

He tested this hypothesis with clients and "within 90 days of his arrival, Mr. Gerstner irrevocably decided to keep the company together" and to concentrate on integrated global solutions. He collected only the data that he needed to test his hypothesis rather than all the data available about the pluses and minuses of the federation model. Then he designed a solution that fit his conclusions and the capabilities of the organization: to "build this company from the customer back, not from the company out."

Al Morrison is a vice president with twenty-six years of experience at A. T. Kearney, a global management consulting organization. He believes that "the process really shines when you don't have time to do all the boil-the-ocean analyses. An 80 percent solution today is usually more valuable than a 100 percent solution next week."

He got a call one Super Bowl Sunday afternoon asking him to go to Chicago the next day to help an organization with a corporate restructuring. The solution had to be presented to the company's board of directors at the beginning of March. Clearly, there was no time to waste. When Morrison arrived on Monday morning, there were 2,500 employees at corporate headquarters. One month later, there were 280. How did he and his team do it?

Al's working hypothesis was that operating divisions could be more effective—more agile and cost efficient—if they had resources close to them. He answered only three questions to test his hypothesis:

1. What has to happen at corporate headquarters for strategic or governance reasons?
2. Which business units will take over the functions that do not have to be managed centrally?
3. What do we do with the employees who are not necessary at corporate headquarters and will not be reassigned to the business units?

If Morrison had conducted a typical analysis, it would have taken six months. He would have benchmarked other organizations, determined corporate and business unit needs, and conducted a current-state analysis to find out what each of the 2,500 people was doing. It would have taken sixty days just to design the questions, collect the data, and enter the details of the current state into a database. It would have been an interesting exercise, but it was unnecessary to help this organization.

Lori Bremer, a vice president at American Express, has more than eighteen years of problem-solving experience. She is responsible for charge card product strategy and new product development in international markets. She finds that the process described in this book gives focus and direction to all the assignments she undertakes. When I last spoke with her, she was conducting an international product line strategy and said to me, "When you follow the process formally, it's time-consuming. It seems easier to shoot from the hip. Longer term, however, you're less efficient because you often have to rework. . . . We're often criticized for being too process-oriented, but without hypotheses and a plan we'd have anarchy. . . . I have taken my teams through the process and consistently, they find it extremely useful and valuable. It should be part of the basic training curriculum for the corporation. It gives people who are smart and analytical a process to follow. It helps them stay organized."

Until a recent promotion, Hans-Ulrich Mayer was responsible for internal consulting at Nestlé. One of the projects his team worked on was a major rationalization in Asia: ten factories, ten markets, and ten products. He found that the process described in this book helped bring his team together. People from many varied backgrounds and twenty nationalities all developed a common vocabulary and approach to the problem. Mayer told me that they had "improved their productivity in a major way. A more complicated project needs more structure and this process provided it."

It took Mayer quite a while to convince people to learn how to design solutions. As an internal consultant focusing on industrial strategies, he was responsible for deciding where and when to open and close factories. Most members of his group were high performers within the organization with at least five years of industry experience, often in Nestlé's operating companies. Most were also implementers at heart and had a natural suspicion of methodology. They thought it would add unnecessary bureaucracy without sufficient benefit. Mayer made them try it.

Hans-Ulrich has now completed eighty projects using the process set out in this book. Without the process, he feels he would not have been as successful as he has been—a success that is corroborated by his career progression.

Kenneth Lay worked for IBM for twenty-seven years and is a senior vice president at JP Morgan Chase. He learned about structured problem solving when he was at IBM and has used it ever since. He finds that the greatest challenge in the approach is convincing others that process, structure, and discipline are the best way to solve problems. "The use of this process ought to be intuitive, but for lots of people, it isn't. Its benefit comes from the discipline it forces on the problem solvers."

The Details

Designing Solutions for Your Business Problems is divided into three parts that follow the path of a typical project (see Figure I.1). In addition to the process steps, you must build relationships, nurture commitment, and drive execution throughout a

FIGURE I.1 PROCESS DETAILS.

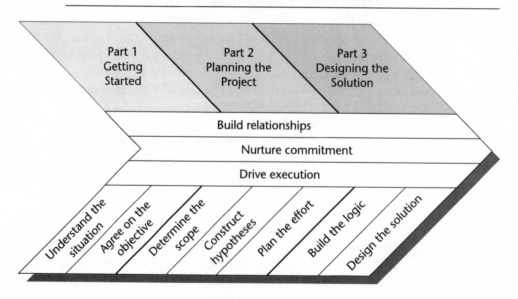

project. Chapters about each of these subjects are interspersed among the process chapters. Each part ends with suggestions for trying out the tools and approaches explored in the part.

Part One: Getting Started

Often the most demanding aspect of solving a problem or investigating an opportunity is understanding the environment in which the solution must work and the organizational constraints imposed upon it. It is a very rare problem or opportunity that isn't subject to a challenging environment. Good problem solvers not only try to think outside the box; they begin by understanding the box better. Chapter One provides you with tools to help you consider the situation you are facing as an integrated whole at the outset of a project rather than a series of impediments you encounter throughout.

Chapter Two explores why specific objectives are much more likely to be effective than vague statements of purpose. The objective is the desired result, not the activities to be undertaken. For example, developing a strategy is not an objective. Developing a strategy in order to improve performance by 10 percent during the next year is. In addition, an objective has to be the aim of the person for whom the project is being undertaken, not the person who is doing the work (unless, of course, you are your own client).

The beginning of a problem-solving project is often a stressful time for all the participants. People may not know each other very well, expectations may be unclear, and ground rules for how individuals will work together have not been set. To make the situation even more challenging, the process by which people sort through these issues may determine the tenor of their relationships. Chapter Three identifies the important elements of communication during the early stages of a project and how you can build relationships to sustain you and the group through the challenging times ahead.

Part Two: Planning the Project

Even with a clear objective, there is often a great deal of debate concerning the scope of a project. You have to quickly define and reach consensus about the areas that will be investigated and those that will remain off limits. By applying an understanding of the limitations of human attention and the need to be mutually exclusive and collectively exhaustive, you will find the appropriate balance between inclusiveness and achievability. Chapter Four develops a solid framework to use in the battle against scope creep throughout the duration of the project.

There are a lot more data about any problem or opportunity than you will ever have time to collect and analyze. The sooner you can determine what is relevant, the sooner you will reach a conclusion and be able to implement a solution. Hypotheses organize and limit data collection to that which is most likely to be important and useful. Chapter Five explains the most practical way to decide which data to collect and shows you how to use such information to maximize the benefit of your efforts.

Once you have developed the hypotheses you will use to drive data collection, you can develop a detailed plan of the problem-solving effort. Chapter Six demonstrates how to use planning tools and techniques effectively and connect them to the rest of the problem-solving process.

When solving a problem, you have to start from where the organization is starting, not from where you are or where you would like the organization to end up. You have to go back to your understanding of the situation and its constraints. Coercion and begging do not work. It is important to remember that what people say may not be what they think. Often "yes" means, "I'm tired of all this," and "no" means, "I'm not up to the risk or effort." You must provide understanding and motivation; commitment and action are up to the doers. Chapter Seven describes how to get commitment from key stakeholders and explores the challenges and opportunities associated with bringing people along during the problem-solving process. It also provides advice on structuring communications whose main purpose is learning rather than informing or selling.

Part Three: Designing the Solution

Once you begin collecting data, you also begin developing opinions about what the organization should do. These opinions start to give you a sense of your conclusions about the problem or opportunity, which helps to lead you to decisions and probable solutions. The challenge in all of this is keeping everything straight. Which hypotheses should you accept? Which ones should you reject? Which ones require you to gather more data? Which data are useful? Which are trustworthy? Why are there inconsistencies? Do they matter? You need to move from a morass of inconsistent and unclear data to a set of clear and logically consistent conclusions that lead to innovative and practical solutions. But how should you do this?

Chapter Eight explains the logic diagram, the core of the problem-solving process. A logic diagram shows the connections among the data you gather, the findings you deduce from the data, the conclusions you reach based on the findings, and the solution you recommend based on your conclusions. It allows you to test quickly whether the argument you hope to use to convince others to act is both complete and consistent. Each component can be tested by itself, but it is testing the whole that enables you to determine whether you are really making any sense.

Your first idea is rarely your best. Often, people have the mistaken notion that they should go with their first hunches. The reality is that a first idea to solve a problem has nothing more going for it than the fact that it was the first idea. It is no better than a first draft. Taking the time to consider other options will usually lead to the best solution. But thinking of alternatives once there is an answer available frequently seems like a waste of time. You may be tempted to come up with nothing but straw men once you have developed a solution you are comfortable with. Chapter Nine helps you quickly devise plausible options and then select among them based not only on their elegance, but also on the will and the ability of the organization to implement them.

No matter how involved people are in the development of the solution and how committed they are to its implementation, there is no guarantee that they will follow through and do something. In order to execute, people need to know what to do, why they should do it, and how they should proceed. The solution provides the *what*. Chapter Ten describes *how* to put together a justification that will be understood long after the people who created it have moved on, as well as how to develop an action plan that enables people to implement the solution you recommend.

Appendix A describes how to map organizational processes and the analyses you can undertake to help you understand and assess them. Appendix B describes how to plan, prepare for, conduct, and record data collection interviews. The CD-ROM accompanying *Designing Solutions for Your Business Problems* contains a case study, a process checklist, and copies of the forms and templates found throughout the book. The case study will give you an opportunity to practice the process and compare your solution to the one provided. The process checklist will help you stay organized as you conduct projects, and the forms and templates provide a starting point for documenting your progress.

Designing Solutions for Your Business Problems will introduce you to the steps to manage the problem-solving process. You will begin by understanding the situation and your needs or the needs of your boss or your client. Then you will define the objectives of the project, and determine its scope. You will work with the project's scope to develop hypotheses and the questions to test them. Then you will create a matrix of the data sources you will tap to answer your questions. The matrix, in turn, leads to your project plan. When you have collected the data, you will develop a logic diagram that shows how you have synthesized the data into findings and how the findings have enabled you to draw conclusions. Your conclusions lead to your solution and action plan. While undertaking these steps, you also need

FIGURE I.2. DESIGNING SOLUTIONS TOOL KIT.

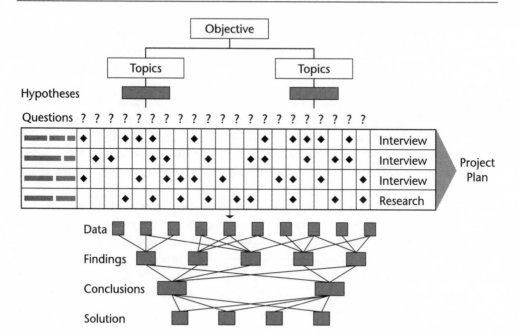

to keep focused on building relationships, nurturing commitment, and driving execution. Over the course of the book, the diagram in Figure I.2 will be constructed piece by piece. You can use it to keep track of your progress.

The real world isn't linear, and it is unlikely that you will ever have a project that will enable you to follow each step one after another without skipping around and backtracking. Your challenge will be to determine how to use the tools and the process effectively to support your problem solving without becoming a slave to them.

PART ONE

GETTING STARTED

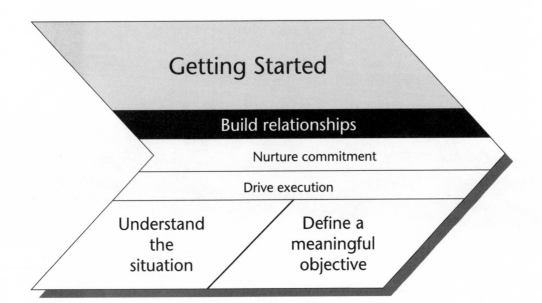

Getting Started

Build relationships

Nurture commitment

Drive execution

Understand the situation

Define a meaningful objective

CHAPTER ONE

ALL PROBLEMS ARE LOCAL

Understanding the Situation

John Savage, an experienced organizational development consultant, was once asked to help the senior management group of a large professional services organization jump-start an implementation. Six months earlier, the group had developed a new strategy, but nothing had happened; there had been no follow-through, and the strategy was languishing.

Before he developed an intervention, John spent time interviewing people across the organization in order to get a better understanding of the corporate situation. He asked them questions about their perceptions and how they felt about the strategy and each other. He found that there was so little trust among the leaders of the firm that they held back opinions and would not share what was on their minds with their colleagues. Many had given lip-service to the strategy, but the group was not open enough to allow disagreements to surface.

Once he understood the situation, John was ready to develop an appropriate solution. He conducted a three-day retreat, with the first two days devoted exclusively to understanding and developing trust. On the third day, the group revisited the strategy and participated in an honest discussion about its merits and shortcomings. Implementation results were much better the second time around.

Had John developed a solution to deal with the problem that was initially presented, it would have been a failure. Without fully understanding the situation, he might have rushed to the assumption that the group needed coaching on implementation and change management. It wouldn't have worked since the primary issue, an absence of trust among the leaders, would not have been resolved. Without first building this trust, other interventions wouldn't have helped the organization move forward.

One of the reasons that companies look to outsiders for help is their independence. They are not caught up in the day-to-day power, politics, groupthink, and myopia that inevitably affect the performance of organizations. However, independence notwithstanding, there is no way to effectively help an organization without understanding the way things work in some detail. When you are an insider solving a problem, you need to stand back and look at your organization as an integrated system rather than focusing on the detail.

Whether you are an insider or an outsider, you must spend time understanding the situation before assuming you have appropriate ideas about changing it. You will want to explore it in all its richness—not just what gets done, but who does it and what they think about it and their respective roles in the process. By understanding what is going on from several perspectives, you have a greater chance of success. Of course, you can never develop a complete picture of the situation, and your picture will never be absolutely objective. Nevertheless, having an incomplete and slanted understanding of a situation is markedly better than having none at all.

To understand a situation fully, you must think about it using several different lenses. Drawing pictures of the relationships among its entities may also bring clarity.

Describing the Situation

The first step to understanding a situation is to bound it. You do this by developing a clear and succinct description of what interests or concerns you. All organizations exist to add value by transforming inputs into outputs. The situation you are interested in will always have at its core a transformation process.[1] Sometimes the transformation is concerned with day-to-day business processes. Sometimes it is a one-time change to the way things are done. For example, if the situation you are facing is that health insurance claim processing costs are too high, the transformation you are interested in is the one that has unprocessed claims as its input and completed or processed claims as its output.

Paying claims is an example of an ongoing business process. Transforming a manual process into an automated one is an example of a one-time change. Both are legitimate transformations with which to be concerned. In the second, however, you have limited the scope of your project because you will not consider options such as outsourcing or elimination. The description of a transformation

FIGURE 1.1. GENERIC TRANSFORMATION PROCESS.

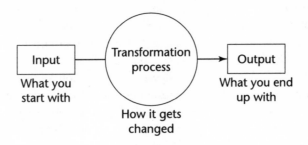

is always expressed as a process in which something (the input) is changed or transformed into a new form of the same thing (the output), as illustrated in Figure 1.1.

You develop a deeper understanding of the transformation by identifying the customers it serves, the activities it comprises, the resources it uses, and the measures that evaluate it. Table 1.1 describes these elements:

Customers

The customers are the people you hope to satisfy—the "beneficiaries or victims" of the transformation.[2] Every activity and process in an organization has customers, whether they are people who buy something from it or the organization or department that must use the output produced. Understanding who they are and what they are thinking and feeling is an important step in maximizing the value of the transformation and any changes you might make to it.

TABLE 1.1. DETAILS OF THE TRANSFORMATION.

Element	Description
Customers	The people you need to satisfy
Activities	The steps of the transformation—the actions that cause it to occur
Resources	People, equipment, and information that are used to make the transformation happen
Measures	The elements of the transformation that you evaluate to ensure that it is working well and accomplishing the right things

Activities

The activities of a transformation describe how it takes place. The task is to break down the transformation process into the key activities it comprises. The challenge is rarely to add detail, but rather to limit it to the steps that fully but succinctly describe the transformation. If that seems shallow, you can always treat each activity as a lower-level transformation and break it down further. For example, if you are investigating the claim transformation discussed earlier, the activities you might consider could include establishing patient eligibility, determining whether a procedure is covered, identifying who should be paid, authorizing payment, and informing the patient and the provider of the decisions.

There are several steps involved in each of these activities. Your judgment is required to determine whether to elaborate on each step to be sure that both you and those you are helping are in agreement on how the claims process works. By diagramming it, you can test your understanding. (Appendix A provides more detail on mapping processes.) In most instances when creating a map to understand a transformation, a simple drawing such as the one in Figure 1.2 is sufficient.

Resources

Resources are the assets that are used to make the transformation happen: employees, purchased services, supplies, equipment, computer systems, and the like. Management reports are a good source for helping you understand the direct resources that a transformation consumes. However, it is also necessary to consider those assets that are used but not consumed during a transformation, such as office space or capital equipment, and those resources that are rarely measured but are almost always constrained, such as top management attention.

FIGURE 1.2. SIMPLE TRANSFORMATION.

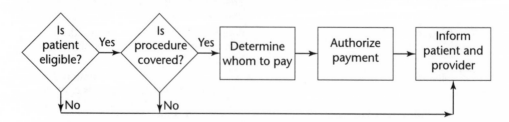

The level of detail you employ in defining resources depends on the nature of the transformation and what you are trying to improve. For example, if you are concerned about employee satisfaction, detail on overhead costs is not nearly as relevant as it would be if you were concerned about operating efficiency.

Measures

A transformation is measured in order to assess whether it is successful. By comparing the measures before and after your intervention, you can determine if you attempted the correct change, whether it was implemented appropriately, and what you should do next. In other words, you learn from the process.

As Figure 1.3 illustrates, the purpose of measurement is to collect data that will enable you to understand what is going on. You can then decide on the best action to take to improve the situation.

There are two types of actions: those that improve the situation as it is currently configured and those that change something fundamental about its makeup. The cruise control on a car provides a simple example. Cruise control keeps a car moving forward at a constant speed regardless of changing road conditions—road surface, wind speed, and topography. It works by taking frequent measurements and then making adjustments based on the results. However, the cruise control cannot change the speed of the car without human intervention. Whether the car is going at the appropriate speed is a more fundamental question than whether it is going at a predetermined speed. An even more

FIGURE 1.3. MEASUREMENT PROCESS.

Analyze Implications
What should be done to improve the results?

Take Action

Analyze Results
Why the result is the way it is.

fundamental question is whether the car is going to the right place at the right time. If you do not ask the questions about speed and direction, they certainly will not change.

It is absolutely critical to think through what the right measurements are for each transformation and to go beyond those that measure what is going on today to include those that gauge whether what is going on *should* be going on. At a minimum, you will want to consider three measures:

- Efficacy, which measures whether a transformation does what it was intended to. In the claims example, do claims get paid, and are they paid accurately?
- Efficiency, which measures whether a transformation uses the least number of resources. In the example, does paying claims take a minimum amount of time and expense?
- Effectiveness, which measures whether the process is doing the right thing. In the example, are you able to pay claims for the customers and product lines that you want to serve? Are you satisfying customers?

Your selection of measures depends on what you believe it takes to make the transformation successful. In order to productively learn about a situation so that you can change it appropriately, you must be clear about criteria to evaluate it.

Understanding the Situation Through Different Lenses

The input-transformation-output definition of a situation is too simplistic for developing a rich understanding of it. The transformation happens in an environment. Someone initiates the transformation, someone could stop it if it didn't meet her needs, someone measures and manages it, someone decides if and when it should be changed and places constraints on how the transformation can and will be performed. You need different lenses through which to view the situation in which the transformation takes place in order to enhance your understanding. Table 1.2 sets out the elements that must be considered.

Worldview

Your worldview is the lens through which you observe all that takes place around you. It determines whether you see the glass as half full or half empty, a challenge as a problem or an opportunity, an individual as a terrorist or a freedom fighter, or wrestling as entertaining or barbaric. In an organizational setting, the worldview

TABLE 1.2. ELEMENTS OF THE SITUATION.

Element	Description
Worldview	The lens through which the transformation is viewed
Environment	Elements outside the situation that should be taken as unchangeable
Social system	The interaction of the roles, norms, and values of the organization
Power and politics	Who holds the power, why they hold it, how they use it, and how they keep it

determines the nature and direction of decisions. For example, in the claims office, there may be a worldview that technology trumps people in terms of efficiency and effectiveness or a worldview that personalized service is key to customer satisfaction. Very different choices would be made in terms of how to improve operations depending on the worldview in place.

With the first worldview, all processes would be streamlined so they could be automated, and it would be difficult for a customer to talk to a human being. In the second, a person rather than a voice response unit might answer the phone. Worldviews are surprisingly robust. An organization's worldview can change over time, but it rarely changes quickly or as the result of a single intervention. Hence, understanding the organization's worldview is paramount to developing options that are acceptable and that can and will be adopted. In some situations, you may believe that the worldview is the problem or provides the opportunity. Understanding what it is and how ingrained it is in the organization will give you insight into how challenging it may be to alter.

Environment

The environment consists of everything that occurs around and affects the project situation but is unchangeable by it. It defines the boundaries of the project. For example, the environment might dictate that a particular technology must be used, that the organizational structure is not to be altered, that the return on an initiative must exceed 14 percent, or that the analysis will not extend to manufacturing. In addition to organizational rules and mandates, the environment may encompass the competition, customers, suppliers, regulatory agencies, and government.

There is always the possibility that you need to challenge the environment and the boundaries it places on the project in order to be successful. Understanding exactly what those boundaries are is the critical first step.

Social System

Transformations occur within the culture of an organization. The ways in which people relate to one another and to the situation have as much to do with a transformation's success or failure as the activities comprising it. In addition to being desirable, any changes to a situation must be culturally feasible. A key component of an organization's culture is its social system, which consists of the constantly changing interaction among the roles, values, and norms of its members.

Roles are the social positions that people involved in the problem situation recognize as important. Rather than organizational positions, they are defined in terms of the primary behaviors or activities associated with those positions. A manager may play the role of teacher, mentor, organizer, or evaluator. A customer service representative might be portrayed as a problem solver, confidant, cheerleader, or salesperson. Each portrayal says something different about what is important to the success in the position and for the organization overall.

The way that roles are carried out is defined to a large extent by the *norms* of the organization—the way that people are expected to behave. For example, some organizations have an expectation that e-mail is answered within a half-day, while others don't expect responses that quickly.

Performance in a role will be judged by the *values* of the organization. In some organizations, responding quickly to e-mail is a sign of diligence and being on top of your duties. In others, it indicates that you do not have enough to do or have not taken the time to think through your response carefully.

You are unlikely to get good answers if you ask people directly about roles, norms, and values. Instead, you have to keep your eyes open to what is going on around you and collect data to help you make inferences. For example, the cleanliness of the facilities and the relative cleanliness of customer areas compared to the rest of the building are indicative of the values of the organization. How hard it is to get a cup of coffee and whether chatting is tolerated also illustrate organizational priorities. I once worked with a company in which photographs and other personal items were not allowed; the way the office looked was more important than the personalization of space.

When Louis Gerstner became the chairman of IBM, the standard process for all meetings was to show transparencies on an overhead projector, much as PowerPoint is the norm at many companies today. At one of the first presentations he attended, Gerstner turned off the projector after the second transparency and asked the presenter to "just talk about your business." E-mail ensured that the whole organization got the message—that day! On another occasion, Gerstner directed IBM aircraft to carry liquor, breaking a long-standing policy that did not permit alcohol on IBM property. In 1995, he relaxed the dress code. It was clear to everyone that form was no longer as important as substance. The culture of the organization began to change decisively.[3]

Power and Politics

An organization's culture is affected by its power structure. Power and politics are generally related to the organizational chart, but are more complicated and nebulous than any chart could depict. Without an understanding of the power and politics of an organization, it is exceedingly difficult to get anything accomplished, particularly to make complex changes. Your objective in analyzing these aspects of culture is to understand how power is obtained or bestowed on people, how people use it to accomplish their aims, how they maintain and protect it, and how and if they can pass it on.

Power is either positional or personal: people acquire power because of their position in the organization or because of their personal attributes. Positional power includes the obvious formal authority that supervisors have over their direct reports. However, it also includes other aspects, such as relevance, centrality, autonomy, and visibility.

If someone is in a position that is relatively more important to the success of the organization, that person has more power. For example, in most brokerage houses, people who sell are considered more important than people who conduct research.

A person with a central position in an organization may have informal power that his job title doesn't indicate. In most organizations, the CEO's administrative assistant is a person with that sort of power. Another example might be a person to whom many people come for advice.

Autonomy bestows power when people can choose the projects or tasks on which they will work. Many research and product development organizations have this sort of power.

Finally, visibility bestows power. In one organization, a group of new employees, just out of graduate school, work as consultants for the president. These people are perceived as having much more power than they deserve based on their expertise and tenure with the company. As a consequence, it is easier for them to get the time and attention of the departments and divisions they serve.

Personal power is more difficult to identify but no less real. Typically, personal power derives from an individual's expertise, track record, extent of effort, or level of charisma. In general, experienced people have more power than those with less experience. People with a longer track record have more power than people with a shorter track record, and people who work smart have more power than people who work hard. Charisma is harder to quantify, but we all know it when we see it. Finally, power is manifested through the will and skill to make decisions. Managers responsible for making decisions lose power if they are unwilling or unable to make them.

As with the social system, it is difficult to ascertain how power works in an organization by asking directly. There is reluctance on the part of many people to openly acknowledge the processes of power. There is also a great deal of inaccuracy and supposition inherent in their thoughts. Sometimes opening a discussion about power changes who has it. Hence, although it is fundamental to the working of any organization, it is often difficult to accurately capture the way power operates. Nevertheless, it is important to try.

Paying attention to whose words are heard and whose ideas get repeated helps you understand power and influence. Whether the leader always sits at the head of the table in meetings is also revealing. In fact, where people sit in meetings tells you a great deal. If they always sit in the same place, there is a clear set of relationships that they are protecting. Similarly, who comes in together and who leaves together can be very telling of connections.

William Johnson, an occupational psychologist turned management consultant, was once asked to reengineer a catalogue operation's order processing. When he arrived at the gate, the guard asked him to park about five hundred yards from the front door. But it was pouring rain, so William asked if he might park in one of the four empty spaces right in front of the building. He was told, "No, the chairman wants those slots for his special guests. He checks twice a day to make sure they're empty." William responded, "Surely you mean his assistant checks the spots?" "No, he does."

William surmised, correctly it turns out, that micromanagement and a lack of flexibility would make it almost impossible to change anything about this organization. If the chairman did not want something to happen, it wouldn't.

Drawing Pictures of the Relationships

Language alone is very limiting in its ability to describe situations. Drawing a diagram of the relationships within an organization often brings increased insight. Most organizations are described pictorially on an organization chart. Although you may be tempted to begin with that because it is good for understanding functional responsibility, an organization chart misses many key factors. It does not describe process ownership. It does not describe the nature of the relationships illustrated and cannot convey who speaks to whom. It fails to connect the organization to its customers and suppliers. And it gives no indication of the feelings that people in the organization have about each other or about you.

Rich pictures help depict what is really going on. A rich picture is "an expression of a problem situation compiled . . . by . . . examining elements of structure, elements of process and the situation climate."[4] In its simplest form, a rich picture is nothing more than circles representing people or departments in an organization connected by lines that signify the relationships they have with one another. Figure 1.4 is an example of such a picture. It describes who talks to whom and the information they share.

A rich picture becomes much more telling when it describes the nature of the relationships among the people involved: the topics about which they communicate, their personal feelings about each other, and their individual concerns. It can portray the social system and the political structure in an organization. It is completely flexible and can be used to describe any situation. There are no rules about what should or shouldn't be included. Figure 1.5 is a rich picture that describes the relationships among the senior management of a small magazine publisher. Figures 1.6 and 1.7 are two pictures of the same situation: a bank whose

FIGURE 1.4. RICH PICTURE OF A BUILDING SUPPLY MANUFACTURER'S RELATIONSHIP TO ITS CUSTOMERS.

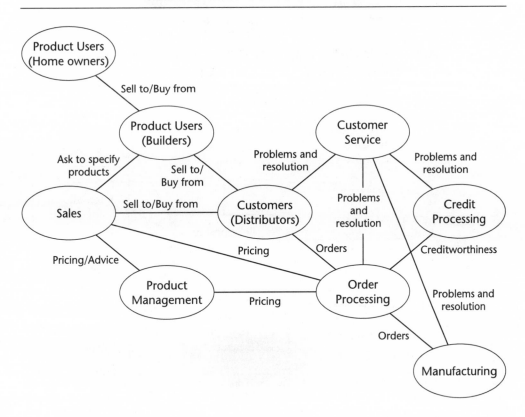

FIGURE 1.5. RELATIONSHIPS AT A MAGAZINE PUBLISHER.

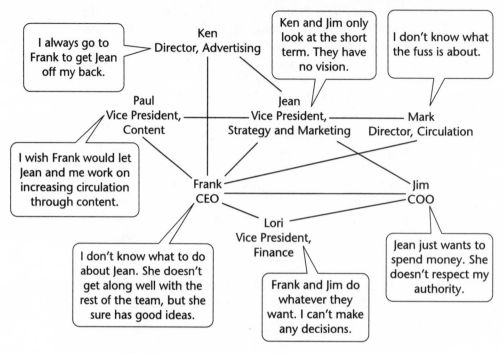

FIGURE 1.6. WHAT SHOULD BE GOING ON AFTER A BANK RESTRUCTURING OF CLIENT CONNECTIONS.

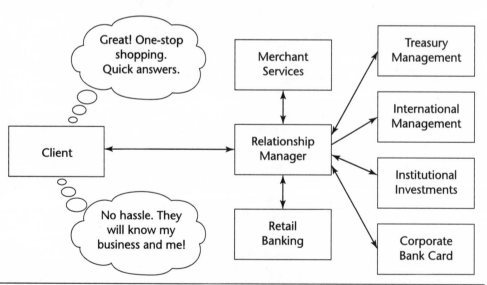

Source: Kevin Gallagher, Derrick Johnson, and Tony Green drew these pictures in 1997 as part of a Systems Analysis and Design class project at the Weatherhead School of Management, Case Western Reserve University.

FIGURE 1.7. WHAT'S ACTUALLY HAPPENING AFTER A BANK RESTRUCTURING OF CLIENT CONNECTIONS.

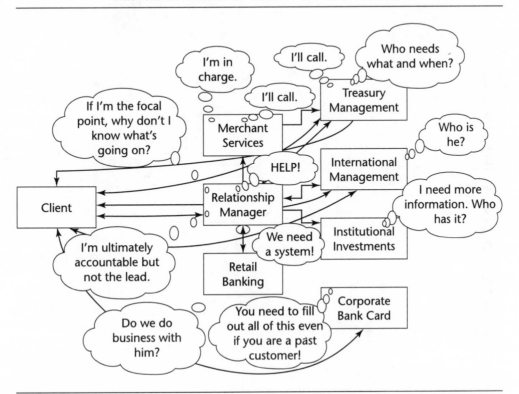

Source: Kevin Gallagher, Derrick Johnson, and Tony Green drew these pictures in 1997 as part of a Systems Analysis and Design class project at the Weatherhead School of Management, Case Western Reserve University.

connections to clients have recently been restructured to go through a relationship manager. Figure 1.6 describes how things should work and Figure 1.7 how they actually do work.

Rich pictures are not limited to balloons and relationships. They can also describe the nature of the relationships and add pictures to make the situation clearer. Figure 1.8 is a more elaborate version of the building supply manufacturer's rich picture shown initially in Figure 1.4. In this picture, you can begin to understand what the organizational units think of each other and how they work, and fail to work, together.

FIGURE 1.8. ANOTHER RICH PICTURE OF THE BUILDING SUPPLY MANUFACTURER.

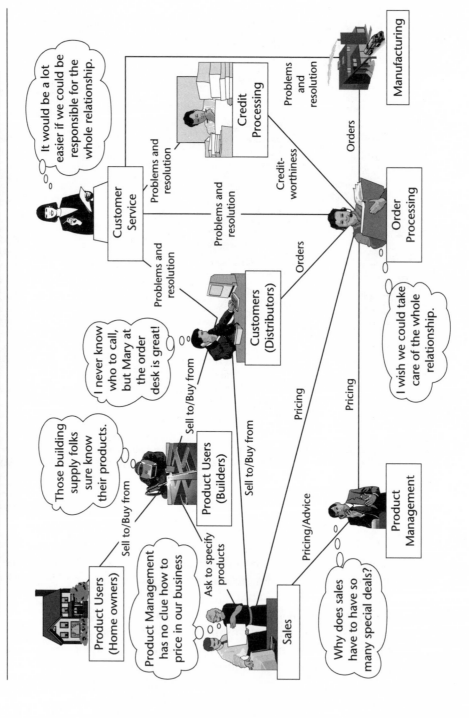

Summary

Why is it important to spend so much time understanding the situation? In most cases, the challenges associated with a project have a great deal to do with what is going on and how people relate to each other. Developing an understanding of these relations makes you more sensitive to what is and what is not possible in the organization with which you are working. It gives you a sense of who to involve when and how to communicate most effectively with them. It helps you to select the right team. Most important, it helps you recognize support and commitment. Knowing how things work today is crucial to understanding how they can be changed.

Once you have a clear understanding of the transformation task you are interested in and the situation in which it happens or will happen, you can define the scope of your project with the confidence that it will be achievable in this particular organization at this particular time.

CHAPTER TWO

WHAT'S THE POINT?

Agreeing on the Objective

A clear and solid objective is the lifeblood of a successful project. Yet many people resist setting specific, measurable objectives, particularly at the beginning of an assignment. Often the reason is that they are afraid of failing. They couch their fear in comments that focus on their lack of knowledge about the situation, the difficulty in being specific, and the need to conduct analyses to determine what is possible.

This chapter describes why formulating specific objectives is much more likely to result in success than relying on vague statements of purpose. It provides a framework that will help you be sure that you understand the specific problem you are solving or the opportunity you are addressing and that you have an objective that is consistent with the problem and also specific, measurable, agreed to, realistic, and time framed. However, before considering your project's objective, you need to be clear about who your client is, who the other stakeholders are, and the nature of everyone's personal agendas. For a project to be successful, the client, as well as the problem solver, has to take ownership of its objective.

The Client

A few years ago, Mike Hastings, a strategy consultant, was asked to conduct a project for a company with two divisions. The head of one division requested the preparation of a quick operations review and a report to the board in three weeks. The managing director of the other division asked for a review of market opportunities. The chairman said, "Those two must be mad. We are totally out of control and need a fundamental assessment of all aspects of our business leading to a strategy and a plan of action." Mike was glad he asked. Had he followed the direction of either division head, he would not have satisfied his client.

An objective is dependent on the person for whom the project is being undertaken: your client. The objective is the result she wants to achieve, not the activities you want to take on. A client cannot be a department or an organization because a department or an organization cannot have, or be held accountable for, an objective. Only people have objectives. In fact, sometimes two people in the same department or organization have very different objectives. Similarly, a department can show signs of opportunity or distress, but exactly what those signs signify depends on the point of view of the person with whom you are talking.

Let's say you are embarking on a project for a credit card call center. There is a vague feeling on the part of senior management that performance needs to be improved. Costs per call are creeping up and seem to be higher than those in the rest of the industry. At the same time, the customers are complaining about the length of time it takes before they talk to a person who can really help them. The call center associates feel they are too pressured to meet quotas to do a good job for the customers. The supervisors want to increase their control over the associates, and the manager wants to be in charge of a larger department in order to increase his power in the organization. Although the wants and opinions of all these people ought to play a role in the solution that is devised, it is probably impossible to satisfy them completely. Consensus may result in the lowest common denominator—usually, do nothing! You need a client to decide and to take ownership of the outcome.

Determining who the client will be is often more challenging than it may first appear. When Paul Lucas was vice president of systems development for Metris Companies, the sixth largest credit card company in the United States, he was asked to develop a system to improve the efficiency and effectiveness of the organization's collections agents. He thought his client was the head of the collections area and had his team build a new system that met her needs. Unfortunately for both Paul and collections, the real client was the head of the systems organization that supported the department. He resisted Paul's solution vigorously because he had an agenda to support the employment of his people and this system would reduce the need for staff in his area. Because the system was under his purview and he would have to pay for and support it, he was the one who ultimately decided it was not right for the organization.

The following questions will help you identify the client:

- Whom do you need to satisfy?
- Who will judge the success of the project?
- Who will fail if the project fails?
- Who has the authority to implement your solution?
- Who will pay the bill?
- To whom will you report?

Stakeholders and Other Interested People

Certainly, the client will be the key person you will strive to satisfy as you undertake your project, but do not ignore everyone else. It is important to understand who has the ear of the client, who can prevent success through neglect or insubordination, and who can champion success through a combination of passion and credibility. Your understanding of the situation as discussed in Chapter One provides a starting point. The people who will affect and be affected by the project will have an enormous effect on how successful you are.

Mike Griffiths, an implementation and change management consultant, was once asked by the senior management of a small oil exploration and production company with a $1 billion market capitalization to help them identify why they had had limited success in finding oil over the previous two years. The CEO suspected the problem had more to do with culture and processes than technical expertise. Mike's team identified reasons for the failures and provided recommendations for action.

Although the conclusions and recommended solutions were robust and ostensibly accepted by the CEO, Mike found out after the presentation that the head of exploration had been using colleagues in the regions to enable him to undermine the outcome of the project. The CEO brushed off the team after the final presentation, saying, "Matters are now well in hand."

Unfortunately, the stock market didn't agree. Once it became clear that the organization wasn't acting to improve its exploration track record, the firm's market capitalization fell by $350 million. One can never be sure about causality when it comes to the stock market, but the correlation was clear. Mike realized that he had ignored the people who had the power to reject the solution and therefore had not solved the problem.

One way to think about people and their relationships to the project and each other is as a series of concentric circles, as shown in Figure 2.1. In the center is

FIGURE 2.1. PROJECT RELATIONSHIPS.

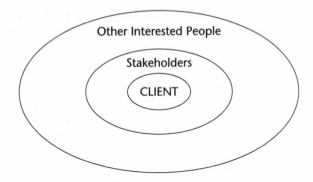

the client. Next are the stakeholders, and finally, in the outside circle are other interested people—those who might influence the project and will be concerned about or affected by its outcome, such as customers, front-line employees, and heads of other divisions. Use your understanding of the situation to arrange the people involved in the transformation in this way. Then test the picture with your client to see if you are right.

The concentric circles approach allows you to illustrate the groupings of people you will be working with on your project. To benefit from identifying them, however, requires a deeper understanding. A stakeholder analysis, with a format like that set out in Table 2.1, keeps track of interested individuals and their goals and concerns. It is a project-specific refinement of your understanding of the organization's context.

Completing the analysis requires you to be observant and sensitive to the situation throughout the project. Ed Wilton, a consultant who specializes in cross-cultural situations, was brought into a pharmaceutical company to help with a cultural change initiative. An American company had purchased two firms, one

TABLE 2.1. STAKEHOLDER ANALYSIS.

Name	Status	Interests, Goals, Concerns
List the names or titles of the project's clients, stakeholders, and other interested people	C—Client S—Stakeholder O—Other interested people; influencers; people affected in some way	Key interests, motivation, goals, and concerns each person has about the project process and expected outcomes

in Germany and one in Italy. The Italians felt aggrieved because they had been merged, and it appeared that the Germans, who were not particularly sensitive to the Italians' needs, were in ascendancy. A weak market, necessitating the rationalization of both products and processes, compounded the problems.

Ed was asked by Human Resources (HR) to help align the new organization. He quickly realized that HR was a barrier to change rather than an enabler. There were two heads of HR who had competing objectives because each wanted to advance his individual power in the new organization. There were also two heads of finance, manufacturing, and engineering. Ed recognized that the managing director of all European operations was the only person who could help to bring the groups together.

Ed and the managing director agreed that the objective for the assignment was to establish a common culture based on communication and the recognition of national differences within the constraints of a nonnegotiable structure and a tight time frame, given the reality of a weak market. The change process required the identification of all the stakeholders—approximately fifteen top managers—who all needed to be heard. Each needed the opportunity to provide his or her personal reaction to the vision and its implications, making clear to the organization what had to change and what they could live with. The next tier of seventy managers, extremely interested parties, were invited to workshops and given the opportunity to express their views and provide feedback to the key stakeholders.

It is unlikely that you will have to keep track of so many stakeholders and interested people in many of your projects. Nevertheless, sensitivity to interests, motivations, and concerns will pay large dividends as you move through the assignment to implementation.

The Objective

When you have determined the client and stakeholders for your project, you can begin to focus on the objective. Remember that the client's objective is not your personal objective. The client is not helped if you look smart or creative. The client is helped if the result of the project is a useful change that gets him to where he wants to go. Answers to three questions will help guide your thinking:

- What does the client want to happen as a result of this project?
- How does this project fit with what else the client is trying to achieve?
- What fundamental question does the client want answered?

Posing these questions to your client directly is not necessarily the best approach. When discussing their problems, individuals often blame symptoms rather than the root cause as the source of their difficulties. When people have a solution in hand, they may seek out the appropriate problem to fit that solution. Determining a fitting objective for a project requires a deep investigation into what is going on. Two stories illustrate.

Not Enough Elevators

In the early 1960s, an insurance company in Boston moved into a new building. Its previous home had been a low-rise structure with very long hallways and only one elevator, which people rarely used. The new building promised to be much more efficient. It was a modern high rise with an elevator core and much less office space per floor. Almost as soon as the company moved, people began complaining about the length of time they had to wait for the elevators to reach their floors. They were of one opinion that the old building had been much more efficient in terms of getting from place to place.

The building managers were appalled. They contacted both the architects and the engineers to find out if anything could be done. Not surprisingly, the engineers assured the managers that the elevators had been calibrated properly and the architects were confident that they had specified the right number of elevators for the number of people in the building. Russell Ackoff, a prominent operations research scientist, was asked to look at the situation. He did so on a Friday and came back the next Monday with a solution: install mirrors in front of the elevators.

Ackoff understood the real problem. It wasn't that it took longer to get from place to place in the new building. In fact, as the architects and engineers had predicted, it took much less time. The problem was how that time was spent. In the old building, people had to walk from place to place, whereas in the new structure, they had to wait for an elevator. Their boredom caused them to perceive the problem to be the time it took to get from place to place, while, in reality, the problem was their boredom itself. Ackoff knew that for most people, time passes quickly when they are looking at themselves.[1]

Too Many Employees

A client called Mike Hastings and said, "Mike, we have to dispense with 115 staff in the field. Where, when, and how are we going to do this?" Mike responded by asking where the number of 115 had come from. It turns out that the finance director was on a cost-cutting binge and had calculated that 115 people would give him the bottom line he was looking for. After a great deal of discussion, the operations manager, the finance director, and the CEO agreed that the real objective was not to cut heads but to reduce overhead costs in the field, the laboratories, and the head office. Increasing the breadth of the project and solving the real problem—overhead, not employees—gave the organization more options and enabled them to minimize the human cost of the reductions.

Although there is no single way to choose an objective for a project and no way to ensure that the objective you have chosen is optimal, it is worthwhile to spend some time understanding potential candidates in order to be more confident that the objective you agree on is appropriate. A few techniques can help: you should be absolutely sure that you understand what the client is saying, you should ask why, you should check that you don't have a solution looking for a problem, you should consider only SMART objectives, and you should agree to work only on something compelling.

Understand the Client

Understanding the meaning of the words a client uses is not trivial. The words used to discuss problems and opportunities are often vague and multidimensioned. Clarity is critical. Without it, you can never be sure that you really understand what the client is looking for.

If the client says, "We need to improve performance," you must first understand what she means by *performance*, then determine whose performance she's talking about, and finally reflect on what would constitute better performance. "Improved performance" could mean increased revenues, reduced costs, higher profits, or faster throughput. Performance could be that of an individual, a department, a business unit, the entire organization, or even the industry. Furthermore, do you have to concern yourself with cannibalization? Is it acceptable to transfer poor performance from one part of the organization to another or from the company to its suppliers or customers?

Why This Objective?

Understanding the "why" of an objective will help to ensure that it is appropriate. While asking "why" five times may seem excessive and more than a bit tedious, it will help you to understand where the client is coming from and whether he is giving you a symptom or a solution rather than a real problem.[2] After all, a problem is nothing more than the difference between what someone perceives to be reality and desired reality. Both are very subjective.

A Swiss clock company is facing increasing costs on its warranty repair line. There are several ways to think about this situation. Someone with a simplistic

view of the situation might investigate the repair process to determine what is causing the cost increases. A more creative person may compare the cost of replacing
the defective clocks with repairing them. The approach that tackles the root cause
would be to determine why clocks are coming back for repairs while under
warranty. In the first case, the problem solver takes the problem as a given and
collects and analyzes data to make a recommendation for improvement. Rather
than spending all that time fixing a symptom, it makes much more sense to get to
the root cause before attempting to solve the problem.

Mike Griffiths faced this type of situation with a global information technology
hardware supplier that was moving into the business of selling services. The head
of operations for Europe wanted to create a stronger focus on services but did not
have clear objectives or expectations for results. He just felt that he needed help.
Mike and his team quickly developed hypotheses about potential problems and
conducted an audit to determine which were real and substantive. They reached
three main conclusions:

- Because there had been little analysis of customer demand for specific services,
  the organization had no clear idea of what the market wanted in terms of
  services and suppliers.
- The sales and service functions did not work closely together, so the sales force
  had no idea what services to sell.
- The primary skills and focus of a services company were missing. This organization focused on technology rather than solving clients' business problems.

Once the head of operations understood the problems he faced, he quickly
conducted several targeted projects aimed at identifying service opportunities,
realigning sales and service, and building skills.

Beware of a Solution Looking for Problems

A solution looking for problems is another trap to avoid. If you agree on an
objective that is nothing more than a solution disguised as an objective, there is
little value in undertaking the effort.

Recall from the call center example that the associates feel they are too pressured by the need to meet quotas to do a good job for customers, while management feels the call center costs too much. Management has decided that the
solution is to ask you to develop a training program to speed up the associates. You
develop and execute the training program, but the associates aren't any faster and
the cost problem persists. It is too late to start asking why, but that is the step you

should have taken at the outset because it may be that the problem is not with the associates. Although they are the largest single expense, they aren't necessarily the source of high costs. Instead, there may be a problem with the technology or with the nature of the questions that customers are asking. Perhaps customers need better information. Perhaps associates need faster access to data. By agreeing to conduct a training program, you have removed all these other possibilities from consideration.

Make Your Objective SMART

The acronym "SMART" can help you judge the quality of your objective. It stands for:

S—Specific

M—Measurable

A—Agreed-to

R—Realistic

T—Time framed

If your objective is SMART, both you and the client will know when you have achieved it. Performance expectations will have been clearly articulated, and results can be measured and agreed on.

If your objective isn't SMART, whether you have done what you were contracted to do is unclear, so it is impossible for you to succeed unequivocally. For example, you may begin with an objective to redesign the process for introducing new products within eight weeks. The good news is that you can't fail: any change to the process during the eight-week period will meet the specifics of the objective. However, if you don't make the changes that your client was thinking about, or if the outcome of the redesign doesn't result in the improvement the client expected, you will not be considered successful. Chances of this happening are pretty high since the objective does not help you to determine either what your client was thinking about or the precise outcome she expected.

The client probably doesn't want a redesign for its own sake. She probably wants the process to be faster, to create higher-quality products, or to lead to faster adoption by customers. Maybe she wants all three. Without being explicit when you set the objective, it is impossible to tell.

The form of a good objective is always the same: it must have an action, it must specify what will be changed, and it must include a measure of success and

FIGURE 2.2. GOOD OBJECTIVE.

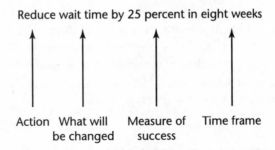

Reduce wait time by 25 percent in eight weeks

Action | What will be changed | Measure of success | Time frame

a time frame. Figure 2.2 provides an example of a thorough objective. Each of the elements is included in the statement, "Reduce wait time by 25 percent in eight weeks." The objective is made specific by being clear about the action and what will be changed. It is made measurable and time-framed by including the measure of success and the time frame in the objective itself.

The value of the measure depends on whether it focuses on organizational outcomes or on process steps. If the measure is about the benefits of the action, it is far superior to a measure that focuses on the effort expended. You want to measure results, not activity. Your understanding of the situation (which you learned how to assess in Chapter One) will help you to determine the appropriate measure for your objective.

An objective is better if it has a time frame than if it doesn't, but it is far better if it is something that can be achieved in a matter of weeks rather than months or years. Many people are taken aback when they hear the possibility of a quick change. Certainly, it takes time to complete some types of projects; for example, many systems development efforts take years to finish. Nevertheless, this reasoning is wrong most of the time. The pace of change in the world today is measured in days and weeks. If it takes you months or even years to respond, you'll never get there. The average lifetime of a technical product is less than eighteen months. An organization that takes two years to implement a strategy to respond to a technical innovation will be left behind.

In addition to the external factors that necessitate the development of short projects, there is an internal reason: people get bored very easily. If they are working on projects that will be implemented soon, there is a much greater chance that they will continue to give it their best. Two shorter and simpler projects back-to-back are more likely to achieve the overall objective than one huge effort that is designed to accomplish the same thing.

Finally, if you shorten the time between the initiation and conclusion of a project, you will find out much sooner if you have been successful. If you haven't been, you can learn from your failure and conceive of and implement another solution more quickly as well.

To determine if an objective is both agreed to and realistic requires discussion with the client and other relevant stakeholders. There is no objective measure in either case. Obviously, more agreement and realism are better than less. Once again, the work you have done to understand the situation will help you assess agreement and reasonableness.

It is hard to make objectives SMART. Following are some examples of objectives that fail the SMART test:

> **Objective: *Complete training of one hundred facilitators on customer service quality within twelve weeks.***
>
> Although this objective is both measurable and time framed, it is not outcome specific. The facilitators can be trained, but nothing else might change. Objectives have to be oriented toward results to be useful.
>
> **Objective: *Improve project management reporting during the next year.***
>
> There is very little chance that this objective will result in failure—or success, for that matter. Some might consider a very small change an improvement, but a very large change might not be enough to obtain the outcomes that others believe the initiative should capture.
>
> **Objective: *Increase call center productivity by 15 percent within eight weeks.***
>
> Determining whether this objective is SMART depends on the organization's definition and measurement approach for productivity. If everyone knows the definition of call center productivity, the objective is fine. If they don't, the objective means very little and is unlikely to bring about success.

Work Only on Compelling Objectives

Beyond being SMART, objectives should be important and compelling. If you find yourself working on a project that has an objective that no one really cares about, you will have a very difficult time completing the project successfully. Even if people agree on the objective, they might not care about it. Change in organizations, or anywhere else for that matter, is sufficiently challenging that you want everything in your favor. People have to care about what you are trying to achieve to make the effort worthwhile. Besides, life is short. Why would you want to waste it thinking about an unimportant problem?

It is not particularly demanding for people to talk about the importance of the issues they ask you to address, but it is more challenging for them to show by their actions that they do think the problem is worthy of attention. John Savage once worked with a client who was insistent that the training John was conducting was absolutely crucial to the success of the organization. John suggested that it would be helpful if someone from senior management attended at least the opening of the sessions to set the tenor of the effort and to answer questions from the participants. At the first session, a senior manager showed up fifteen minutes late and spent about ninety seconds pointing out the location of the restrooms and explaining why no supervisors were present. (They were too busy.) At John's urging, she spent about three minutes at the second session addressing the importance of the program in addition to talking about the rest rooms and the supervisors. (They were still too busy.) She was too busy to show up for the third session. John decided to cancel the remaining sessions.

It's easy to tell if your project is important to the organization. If it is, your client or sponsor will have a visible presence on the project. He will visit the team room. He will ask how the work is going and care about the answer. He will talk about the initiative every chance he gets. He will manage the reward system to support change if that's appropriate. He will make sure that resources are available when they're needed.

Resistance Is a Fact of Life

Clients, consultants, and project participants all resist objectives. Objectives are frightening because they result in evaluation, which is a risky proposition. Even when you explain that you can't tell if you've succeeded without an objective, people shy away from being concrete. They say they need more time, more resources, or more people to determine the right objective. Asking "why" five times helps. It also helps to remember that the objective can be changed as you learn more about the situation. If, in the middle of the project, you realize that the objective is trivial, unrealistic, or meaningless in solving the problem at hand, you can stop and develop a more appropriate goal. In fact, you should regularly check to make sure your objective is appropriate as you collect data and undertake analyses. You and your client must regularly discuss whether the objective is still agreed to and realistic. Remember too that in business problem solving, absolute precision is highly unlikely. The chance that you get the objective exactly right from the start is remote. However, endlessly preparing to begin won't get you anywhere, and beginning without knowing where you want to end up will result in nothing but frustration. Knowing your objective saves both time and energy.

Summary

Setting a good objective is crucial to a successful project, but it is hard to do. Sometimes the client is the problem. He may have too many objectives that are too far out in the future, or that are too vague and not measurable. It's up to you to help him understand why it's important to be more concrete and then to help him become so. Without a good objective, neither of you will be happy at the end of the project.

Sometimes *you* are the problem. Your objective might be to undertake a particular kind of assignment, to use a particular technique, to get more business. If the objective is focused on what you will do or produce rather than the result for the organization, it is unlikely to be compelling.

Unless you have a SMART objective that is important and compelling, you may be better off not moving forward at all. In addition, important and compelling have to be heartfelt. More people than just the project sponsor must care about the objective and want to work toward it. Of course, not everyone has the luxury of walking out when there is no consensus about the importance of a project. If this is the situation you face, your first challenge is to understand why and find out what it would take to make the project worthwhile. It is a rare case in which resistance or apathy dissipates spontaneously. Without deep support, success will be elusive.

If done well, the process of setting an objective has the following benefits. It:

- Creates a link between organizational goals, the client objective, and team member actions
- Creates a social contract of mutual expectations between you and the client
- Provides the foundation for assessment of performance and client satisfaction
- Focuses on moving forward rather than endlessly getting ready to begin

Even with an important and compelling objective, however, a solid relationship with your client is key to achieving the result you are both hoping for.

CHAPTER THREE

PEOPLE HAVE TO BE INTERESTED

Building Relationships

The beginning of a project is often a stressful time for everyone involved. You may not know each other very well, expectations have not been articulated, and ground rules for how you will work together have not been set. You may not even be sure with whom you will work. To make the situation even more challenging, the manner in which you sort through these issues may determine the tenor of your relationship for the entire project. Don't panic. Remember that the situation is new for everyone, and all participants share the same sorts of concerns.

There are three people-oriented tasks that must be accomplished at the outset of a project. First, everyone must understand what the project is about and how it will be conducted. Second, individuals must develop a clear understanding of their roles and how they will contribute to its success. Finally, it is important to foster high-performance working relationships. Normally, you are able to accomplish these tasks through a combination of individual discussions and a kickoff meeting. Although the exact form and substance of discussions and meetings vary from situation to situation, client-focused tips provide the framework for planning these early encounters in a project. Coupling adherence to the tips with well-thought-through and comprehensive communication plans will help you meet your client's needs and the project's objectives.

The Tips

The beginning of the project is when you have the opportunity to set the communication pattern for the entire assignment. How you begin is often how you finish. For the assignment to be successful, you want to be sure that your client believes that you have her best interest at heart and that she trusts you to help her get the job done.

Recently, I had the opportunity to talk with a former consulting colleague and also with his client on a process improvement assignment. I spoke with each of them individually about the nature of their relationship (I have changed their names here for confidentiality). Jim, my colleague, felt the relationship had gotten off on the right foot because, he said, "I disabused Heather of the idea that this project would be finished in a few months." He also made it very clear that he was helping, but that Heather owned the problem and was going to have to see it through to resolution. Then he described a situation early on in the assignment in which Heather asked him to conduct an analysis that was only tangentially related to the project. She told him that he was the only one she trusted to do a good job. Although Jim was happy to help Heather in this instance, he pushes back when he thinks her requests are out of line. However, he says that they rarely are. "She doesn't take advantage of our relationship."

Heather was very clear about why she liked working with Jim: "Right from the start, he let me know what I could expect. He didn't sugar-coat the news. He told me the project was going to take longer than I had hoped. We have developed a good relationship—not because Jim works on it but because he works on getting our problem solved. I trust Jim to do what's best for us."

Interestingly, Jim felt that the substance of this particular project was "occasionally interesting," while Heather believed that it offered "great challenges" to the consultants. The difference of opinions didn't matter. The project was important and compelling for Heather, so Jim was eager to support her and help her reach her objective. Both are happy with the way the work is going, and both are confident that the project will succeed.

Several lessons can be drawn from this positive relationship. First, during my interviews with each of them, it became clear to me that the most important element of their mutually beneficial relationship is trust. Jim trusts Heather to own the problem and take his advice, and Heather trusts Jim to advise her appropriately. Before trust can develop, however, competence and intent must be established. If Jim had not provided a robust and compelling early analysis, even if he had had the best of intentions, Heather's trust would have diminished. In every situation, it is crucial that you are realistic about your capabilities and that you deliver what you promise. Trust is much harder to repair than to establish. In addition, establishing trust might mean that you have to give something away. Offering to help someone without expecting something in return shows you care and really do want to help, but only if you are sincere and truly do not expect a quid pro quo in the future.

Defining expectations at the outset of the project helped Jim and Heather's relationship work smoothly. Heather did not intimidate Jim. Jim did not conceal the initial bad news that he had. He was straightforward and honest in all their dealings. Jim made it clear to Heather what he expected of her as a client, and she not only promised to deliver but followed through on those expectations. Openness and integrity are fundamental and are particularly important to establish early in a relationship.

Third, and perhaps most important, Jim and Heather did not focus on building their relationship. They focused on getting the job done, and the relationship built itself. This is not to say that they don't enjoy working together; they do. Both have a great deal of respect for each other's capabilities and empathy for each other's challenges. And they are considerate of one another's time and do not take advantage of each other.

Here are a few more tips, in addition to those that emerged from my description of Jim and Heather, that contribute to building the respect and trust required for an effective client–problem solver relationship:

- *Make winners of everyone.* It is much more important to get the job done than to get credit for getting the job done. Work to ensure that members of the client organization have an opportunity to use their own words in reports and that they, rather than the problem solvers, make presentations whenever possible.
- *Get feedback and advice.* Listen. Your client knows more about the organization than you do. Get her help. If you think you've seen this situation before, you're wrong.
- *Manage expectations.* If you are clear about what is possible and agree on what is to be accomplished, the chance of disappointment is much less. Don't cave in to expectations that will take the assignment out of scope or that can never be met.
- *Avoid surprising the client.* Bad news doesn't get better with age.
- *Learn from your experiences.* Find out which communication approaches work best in this organization, and use them.
- Throughout the project, but particularly early on, *control your excitement.* Don't overpromise, and always deliver what you promise. Don't deliver "first blush"

good news before you have verified it and don't overdeliver early on unless you are sure you can maintain the pace throughout the project. Remember that consistency often earns more points than the occasional flash of effort or insight.

- *Build in involvement.* Involvement consists of more than token participation at meetings; it is defined by an individual's willingness and ability to contribute to the decision-making process. It is your challenge at the outset of a project to let people know you care about what they think and that you will continue caring until the end of the assignment and beyond.

- *Don't show off.* If you have to tell people how great you are, you're probably not all that great.

The Communication Plan

Communication is simple: don't focus on what you want to say; focus on what your audience, whether it consists of one person or one hundred people, is ready for and needs to hear.

The purpose of any communication is to elicit a response. Your task is to create the right message and send it to the audience using the right medium, motivating them to respond or take action. Every communication is really a project in microcosm. You need to understand the situation, develop an objective, and determine the best way to meet it, given the situation. As in the project overall, you begin with a plan. Table 3.1 lists the elements that you ought to consider.

Objective

A communication objective should be the response you hope to trigger in the receiver. Obviously, an objective for a specific communication is not as grand as one for an entire project, but it does share many of the same characteristics. It ought to be concise as well as outcome specific—for example, "As a result of this meeting, the CEO will elicit support from the vice presidents." This objective is much more challenging than, "As a result of this meeting, the CEO will find out that we would like her to elicit support from the vice presidents."

It is easy to tell if the first objective has been met. The second is more tenuous. After all, she might not have been listening. Here are some other examples of clear and measurable communication objectives:

> "As a result of this conversation, the department will provide insight into the problems with product enhancements."

TABLE 3.1. ELEMENTS OF A COMMUNICATION PLAN.

Plan Element	Considerations
Objective	The response or action you want to elicit from the audience; what you want them to do
Audience	Role (decision makers, opinion leaders, influencers) Group and individual characteristics Receptivity and motivation Culture and expectations
Message	Emphasis Order
Medium	Control Formality Permanency Detail Feedback Richness Efficiency
Value to the audience	A succinct description of the value of your communication—not to you, but to your audience

Source: Adapted from Munter, M. *Guide to Managerial Communication.* Upper Saddle River, N.J.: Prentice Hall, 2000.

"As a result of this e-mail, staff will collect the necessary data about the Oxford Street location."

"As a result of this discussion, we will generate some creative alternatives."

"As a result of this presentation, the clients will get to know us and feel comfortable with our approach."

It is important to remember that the objective for each communication should help you move toward your project objective.

Audience

As individuals, members of your audience will each have their own opinions, interests, expectations, and attitudes. As members of a group, they will have norms, standards, and values. How you respond to their expectations will determine how well they listen. Beyond understanding their expectations, you should develop a sense of what they know so you can identify gaps in the information they have received. Following are some questions you might ask yourself and some comments on them:

- *How much background information do they have? How much new information do they need?* It's insulting and patronizing to be told something you already know and insulting and intimidating not to have enough background to understand what is being discussed.
- *What are their expectations and preferences in terms of communication style, length, and format?* There's nothing wrong with trying to shake people from their habits, but don't do so by accident. Trying something unexpected is risky. Make sure it's a worthwhile risk.
- *How interested are they in the message and the objective?* If they are interested, it will be easier for you to communicate your message. If they aren't, you will need to engage them before you can begin to focus on your communication objective. Often, you can foster buy-in by involving people in the communication process. Anyone who shares control of the communication will have a greater interest in the outcome of the effort.
- *What is their probable bias?* If their bias is negative, it usually makes sense to make your requests as small as possible. You will be more likely to obtain buy-in if you state the points of agreement first and then respond to anticipated objections. It also helps if you explain why you rejected opposing arguments.
- *Is your requested action easy or hard? How are they are likely to feel about it?* Are they dissatisfied with the status quo, or are they complacent and resistant to change?
- *Are they afraid, or are they excited?* Emotional needs are just as important as intellectual needs and you have to respond to both. Physical needs are also critical, but those are much easier for most of us to satisfy. Nevertheless, someone who is too hot, too cold, too hungry, or too tired is less likely to be actively engaged in the communication.
- *What might motivate them to act?* Will they respond only if they will benefit personally? Will they respond to your credibility?

Message

Your communication objective and the characteristics of your audience will provide you with the insight to determine the content of your communication. You have to decide what you will emphasize and how you will order it. Since human beings do best with a logical progression, you have only a few choices. Do you want to begin with an overview and work down to the necessary detail, or do you want to begin with the detail and build up to your point? Starting with the overview is the most natural way to present information, but it can become laborious if the audience is impatient to get to the point. Starting with the details is rarely a good idea because the audience doesn't have a context to connect the details to. It's like giving someone crossword puzzle clues without the grid to fill in. However, if the audience is very negative or insecure, it may be a gentler way to get to the point. For most business communications, neither is particularly effective without a headline. It is usually best to begin with your main point and then provide support for it by building up the detail or breaking down the overview.

Medium

Many communications happen without a great deal of thought given to the medium used. People tend to use the media they are used to and those that their audiences expect. In some organizations, people wouldn't dream of going to a senior management meeting without a PowerPoint presentation; in others, the CEO won't read anything that's more than a page long. However, different media have vastly different attributes and different applications for which they are appropriate. You should consider a number of attributes when you are choosing a medium.

Control. How much control do you want over the pace and order of the communication? If you make a formal presentation, you have much more control than if you have an informal hallway conversation. Control lets you determine the order of the message, but it limits the audience's involvement and perhaps their buy-in. Of course, control is determined in part by the audience as well. Sometimes even if you have a formal presentation prepared, it is very difficult to prevent the audience from roaming wherever it wants through questions. If you request that people who are accustomed to asking lots of questions save them, you may miss important interactions.

Formality. Formality is closely related to control. When you stand up, your presentation is more formal than when you sit down. A room set up in classroom style is more formal than a conference table; a letter is more formal than an e-mail. Be sure you want what formality offers. It will make you seem more sure, less receptive to comments and criticisms, and either more respectful or more pompous, depending on the audience. If you are communicating preliminary thoughts, you might be better off with a less formal medium.

Permanency. Do you want a record of the communication? With a conversation or a presentation, all that remains is people's notoriously unreliable recollection and their frequently incomplete notes. With a written report or an e-mail message, the record remains even if you don't want it to.

Detail. How much information must be conveyed, and how detailed is it? Sales statistics are not handled well with a telephone call unless you have only a few numbers to pass on.

Feedback. Some media are much more likely to elicit feedback than others. In general, people would rather talk than write and can process written information faster than spoken. A conversation is a much easier way for someone to respond to your ideas than an e-mail message, but an e-mail message is a faster way for them to get information than a voice mail. People tend to say more in a face-to-face conversation than they do in a telephone call.

Richness. Richer media are those that offer more ability to develop understanding over a shorter period of time.[1] The richer the medium, the better it enables relationship development and collaboration. The reasons for richness differences include speed of feedback and the number of channels used. The richest medium is face-to-face communication because it provides immediate feedback using many senses: hearing, sight, and sometimes touch. Facial expressions and body language provide many clues about point of view that are unavailable over the telephone. You can change your communication in response to the feedback you are receiving as you go along. The telephone is richer than e-mail because it provides voice inflection as well as message.

Efficiency. All other considerations notwithstanding, efficiency also comes into play. Getting people together has many benefits, but it costs more in terms of time and sometimes travel expense. A telephone call costs more than an e-mail message, for example.

Value to the Audience

You will want to think about what value the communication has to the audience. This value is not the same as the value associated with the objective; rather, it is what you promise to deliver to the audience during the meeting. For example, you cannot deliver a profitability increase during a meeting. Hence, a meeting's value is not, "This plan will increase our profit by 15 percent." Rather, it is, "I will show you how we can increase our profit by 15 percent." The value tells your audience why it is worth their while to pay attention.

The Stakeholder Analysis

The stakeholder analysis is a key tool to use throughout your communication planning. When you develop it at the outset of your project, you rarely have significant insight into individuals' preferences and motivations. Nevertheless, it is the best information you have, so you ought to use it to develop your initial plans. For example, if you hear that a particular vice president is unsure about the need to investigate his area of responsibility, set up an early meeting with him and make an effort to delve into his concerns and understand them fully. Your objective for this meeting might be to introduce the vice president to the team members, help him understand the approach you are taking, and learn the background of the organization's decision to seek out the assistance of a consultant. The value you would propose to him at the outset of the meeting might be as follows: "By the end of our hour together, you will have the information you need to assess whether our involvement is right for your organization."

At the end of the meeting, you will have further insight into this person's interests, goals, and concerns. By updating the stakeholder analysis with this information, you can chart your understanding of these details for use in your next interaction with him or his colleagues.

Summary

Initial communications in a project need not be convoluted or complicated. By focusing on the project objective and making sure everyone is informed, involved, and comfortable, you have the best chance of developing the relationships you need to design an effective solution for the situation at hand. If you communicate well and sincerely, by the time the project nears completion, it may no longer be clear whose solution is being recommended, but everyone will be sure that it is right.

USING THE TOOLS

Although you may not be starting a project right now, there are several ways that you can use the tools described in Part One to practice and to help you in your day-to-day work:

- Describe the elements of the situation in your current job.
  What is the transformation in which you are involved?
  What resources do you use, and in what activities are you engaged?
  What are the environment and your organization's worldview?
  What is the social system, and who has the power?
  How do you measure yourself?
- Draw a rich picture of a situation about which you have some concerns. Draw another picture of how someone else might perceive it. Think about why the pictures are different.
- If you are working on a project or have recently completed one, conduct a stakeholder analysis.
  Have you clearly identified the client?
  Are you paying enough attention to everyone who is important?
- If you are working on a project, ask everyone on the team to write down its objective. Compare the responses to each other and to the requirements of SMART.

How consistent are you?

Do the inconsistencies matter?

How SMART is your objective?

Can you improve its specificity and measurability?

Does everyone agree to the objective, and is it realistic?

What do you think about the time frame?

PART TWO

PLANNING THE PROJECT

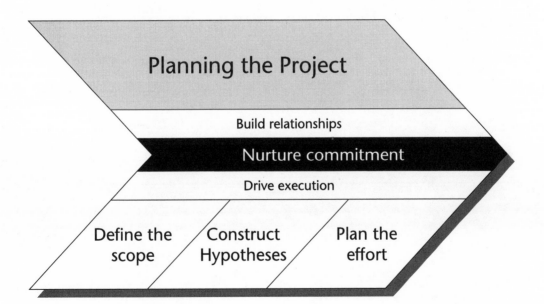

CHAPTER FOUR

SIZE MATTERS

Determining the Scope

Once an objective has been agreed on, your next step should be to define the project's scope. Scope is the opportunity for action and the breadth of a project's reach. It is shaped by the constraints and conditions placed on the project and is dependent on its objective.

Scope is difficult to establish. People's understanding of what is part of the project seems to vary from day to day, and usually in favor of doing more, not less. The only antidote is to work with your client to achieve clarity and focus. Creating a diagram to describe scope helps people to understand a project's boundaries more precisely.

This chapter describes how to think about constraints and conditions and provides a technique for diagramming the scope of your project in order to facilitate discussion and agreement on the project's parameters.

Although agreeing on the objective and determining the scope are described sequentially, often these activities occur in parallel. As you come to understand the scope required to meet your objective, you may decide to refine it, which then changes the scope.

Constraints and Conditions

It is difficult for an organization to take on an overly ambitious project, even if it provides a return commensurate with its risk. Usually the client wants to move from his current situation to another place that he perceives to be better and accomplish this goal while using minimal resources. The client may also have very clear ideas about the geography, customer groups, priorities, acceptable alternatives, and risk he is willing to take on to get there.

Chapter One described how to understand the situation. Constraints and conditions are part of the situation and a direct consequence of it, but they are also project specific. The constraints for one objective, for example, may not be the same as the constraints for another. A company may be willing to invest much more in a new product than in one that has been around for ten years, even though the expected return on investment is the same. Therefore, it is necessary to understand constraints in the light of the specific objective you want to achieve.

A focus on constraints does not imply that you should simply acquiesce to them. Rather, it implies that a sufficient identification and understanding of boundaries is required to make choices. What are the constraints? Should they be accepted? Should they be negotiated? Should they be resisted? Should they be ignored? Do they matter?

Your task is to determine which constraints are real and immutable, which are there only because of a fear of change, and which really matter. A client may tell you that you have to limit yourself to a particular product line, and you will have no trouble doing so. However, if a client asks you to limit yourself to a single office in a single region, you might find it difficult to get anything done.

Resource Constraints

Resources fall into four categories: the client or sponsor, people, time, and the budget. It is important to consider your needs and their availability during the project, after the project has been completed and implementation has begun, and once the project has been implemented and life returns to normal. You might want to complete a resource assessment matrix as shown in Table 4.1 to be sure you have considered all resources for all time periods.

All three time frames are relevant to a project's success. For example, a client may be very willing to support an initiative during its strategic development. However, if the project is unable to hold the client's attention once implementation begins or after the initiative has been launched, it may ultimately fail.

TABLE 4.1. RESOURCE ASSESSMENT MATRIX.

Resources	During Project	During Implementation	After Implementation
Client/Sponsor			
People			
Time			
Budget			

Client or Sponsor. You identify client or sponsor constraints by evaluating how much time and attention the project is likely to receive and determining whether it will be enough. How much time will senior managers have available for you during the project? How much time will they devote to implementation? What the leader does affects what everyone else does. If she is not fully engaged, it is unreasonable to expect the troops to care as much as they might if she were. But you should also be realistic about how much of her time she can devote to the project and work within those confines if you can. Senior management time is an organization's scarcest resource.

People. In this category, you should list how many and name which people will be available during all three stages of the project's life cycle. For example, you may find that a key project resource is to be reassigned once implementation begins. You may find that there will be 30 percent fewer people available after implementation, or you may find that there is no one to staff the function you are creating.

Time. This category refers to how much time you have to complete activities throughout the project and during implementation. Time in the context of business-as-usual is more fluid. For some projects, such as a strategy study, it could be your expectation of how long the strategy will be viable. For others, such as a process improvement project, it might refer to the amount of time available to execute the new process.

Budget. The budget is the most obvious constraint. If the project implementation will require more financial resources than the company can risk expending, it may not be possible to implement, even if the situation afterward would be vastly better than it is today. Remember too that capital and operating expenditures are treated differently by managers, accountants, and tax authorities. For example, many boards are more hesitant about increasing head count than buying new technology. Recognize these distinctions as you consider the constraints surrounding the financing for your project.

When completing the resource assessment matrix in Table 4.1, push to understand what or who is imposing the limits. Are they real? Can you change them? Do you need to change them? Will they make a difference to the outcome of the project, or will you be working well within their boundaries?

Nonresource Constraints

Resources are not the only constraints that clients impose on projects. For example, in the early 1990s, when the *New York Times* was looking for ways to improve circulation, it placed a constraint on the solution. Although the newspaper had reached the saturation point in the New York metropolitan area given its editorial approach, that approach was not to be modified. During the course of the project, the team found that there were people all over the United States who wanted to read the *Times* daily but couldn't get local early morning delivery. The solution that the company designed was to develop high-speed printing capability at eighteen locations around the country and build customer service centers that could be accessed from anywhere in the United States at any time, day or night. In effect, the *Times* offered subscribers all the benefits of a local newspaper. Its circulation grew substantially as a result.[1]

Not all constraints are explicit, but that doesn't make them any less real. While working for a major consulting company, Jeremy Raymond worked with a client who seemed disinterested in long-term recommendations. After puzzling over this problem for some time, Jeremy and his team realized that the average tenure of senior managers in the firm was ten to eighteen months. There was absolutely no point in recommending something whose benefits would take longer than eighteen months to realize.

Structuring the Assignment

You have agreed on the objective for the project and understand the constraints and conditions. Now it's time to think about how you will structure the assignment in order to meet the objective. What areas should you focus on, and what outputs will you produce by investigating each of them? There are two ways to determine scope. You can design a scoping diagram, which lays out the topics that you will investigate and the outputs you will produce to meet the objective, or you can construct an issue tree, which organizes anticipated recommendations about how your objective might be achieved.[2]

The Scoping Diagram

A scoping diagram sets the boundaries of a project by displaying the topics and subtopics you will investigate. Figure 4.1 shows the scoping diagram for a project to reduce claim processing time. It looks like a hierarchical organization chart. The top level lists the objective that you have agreed to with the client. This is followed by the main topics you will investigate. Each of these is divided into subtopics that describe the topic in more detail. You could add another layer of sub-sub topics if you believe more detail is warranted.

The scoping diagram shows the client exactly what you intend to pursue in order to meet the objective. It gives you and your client the opportunity to discuss the specifics of the project. Mike Hastings feels that the scoping diagram was the single tool that changed the culture of an organization that he worked with over a period of several years. The internal consulting team he counseled used objectives and scoping diagrams to bring together steering committee members who had widely differing political agendas. Scoping diagrams enabled the team to gain agreement from the committee on what their projects would accomplish. Prior to using scoping diagrams, the group was forced to proceed on the basis of majority rule or the wishes of the most powerful contingent. This always resulted in disaster at the end of a project when arguments typically surfaced about whether the project had covered what was important.

Scoping diagrams are useful only if they are limited to relevant topics and subtopics but at the same time capture all important aspects of the objective.

FIGURE 4.1. SCOPING DIAGRAM.

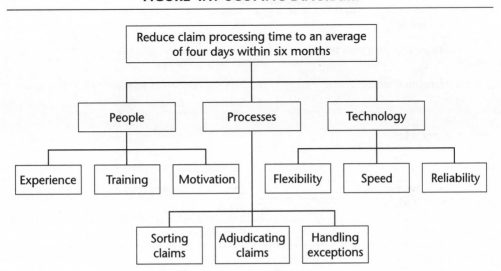

For example, you might agree on an objective to reduce costs by 10 percent within ninety days. Constraints will dictate the exclusion of some topics. There is no point in investigating technology if the client has no control or influence over the technology resources and isn't likely to gain control. Your lack of familiarity with the situation might cause you to omit others that should be included. After looking at a draft of your scoping diagram, the client might indicate that some of the services provided by his unit could be outsourced, but you may not have included outsourcing as a topic for investigation.

Typically, you create a scoping diagram after you have spent some time in the client organization and have done some basic research about the situation the client is facing. If you are going to write a proposal for work to be done, ideally you will complete the scoping diagram before the proposal is written.

Probably the best way to create an initial scoping diagram is to brainstorm possible topics that should be investigated based on what you know about the organization and problems or opportunities similar to the one your client is facing. As with all other brainstorming, the result will be a list of topics that contain various levels of detail and specificity. Your challenge is to organize them into topics and subtopics in a way that clarifies what the project will cover. Following the four guidelines set out in Table 4.2 as you create your scoping diagram ensures that the diagram will be clear, logical, and succinct.

Seven Plus or Minus Two. Human beings have very limited short-term memories. Study after study has shown that most of us cannot remember more than

TABLE 4.2. SCOPING DIAGRAM GUIDELINES.

Guideline	Description
Seven–plus or minus two	Topics cover the objective, but there are no more than seven.
Horizontal logic	The reason for the sequence you choose.
	Each layer contains elements at a similar level of detail or importance to the objective.
Vertical logic	There is a logical trail from objectives to outputs.
	Subtopics are component parts of topics.
Mutually exclusive and collectively exhaustive	Topics are discrete divisions with no overlap.
	All topics taken together completely exhaust the objective.

seven things, plus or minus two, depending on individual intellect.[3] Once we hit our personal limits, we use all sorts of devices to help us remember. For example, most North Americans can look up a seven-digit telephone number, close the book, and dial the number as long as we aren't interrupted during the process. However, in much of North America, the ability to recall seven digits is no longer enough; people also have to remember the area code—a total of ten digits. Most still have no problem. They remember by breaking the number up: 216–255–3324. A British telephone number provides North Americans with greater challenges. North Americans have to remember the digits, and also how many digits there are in each grouping since the 3–3–4 organization doesn't hold. For example, the telephone number 44–1483–22241 seems impossible for the untrained eye and mind to remember.

It makes sense to take this human shortcoming into account when creating a scoping diagram. When there are more than seven topics across the top level of a diagram, it becomes very difficult for anyone to understand it fully because they can't remember the beginning of the list by the time they get to the end.

I believe that when what must be remembered are difficult concepts rather than digits, seven is stretching most of us. My advice is that scoping diagrams should not have more than five topics on the top level. If you find that you have more than five, there is a good chance that you can summarize some of them and add a layer to the diagram. For example, if you decide to organize your diagram according to products, you may have more than five to consider. These can be grouped into product lines or customer groups to simplify the diagram.

Horizontal Logic. Whenever you make a list, you have a choice about the sequence in which you organize it. When most of us go to the grocery store, the list is usually written in the order in which we ran out of items during the week. That's an efficient way to create a list but not a very efficient means of ticking things off. You start in the produce department, but the first item on your list is laundry detergent. Potatoes and onions are somewhere in the middle, and you might or might not notice them before you are standing in the checkout line.

Such a lack of structure is not serious when shopping for groceries, but when you are putting together a scoping diagram, it pays to consider the best way to organize the topics. You may want to put the most important issue first, create your list according to geography, or organize by size. Aside from arbitrarily ordering a list, perhaps the worst way is alphabetically. For example, think about the countries in Europe. Most people are more likely to be able to list them all if they have a map of Europe in their mind's eye than if they have only the alphabet to guide them.

In addition to order, horizontal logic is concerned with scale. Topics or subtopics that are at the same level in the scoping diagram should be of about the same size or importance. For example, if you are undertaking a project to cut costs in the organization, you might list the components of cost at the top level of your scoping diagram: people, facilities, and technology. You should not include a top line topic to focus on paper clips, unless, of course, the main product of the company is paper clips.

Vertical Logic. Vertical logic is concerned with the hierarchy of the scoping diagram. All subtopics must connect to topics, and sub-subtopics must connect to subtopics. Lines do not cross, and many-to-one relationships are not permitted (see Figure 4.2).

In addition to connections, vertical logic is concerned with logical inclusion. Topics that are at a lower level in the hierarchy must be components of the higher-level topics. For example, if the top level of the diagram has sales as a topic, subtopics might consist of sales territories, products, or components of the sales process. They would not consist of steps in the manufacturing process.

FIGURE 4.2. EXAMPLES OF SCOPING DIAGRAMS WITH ERRORS.

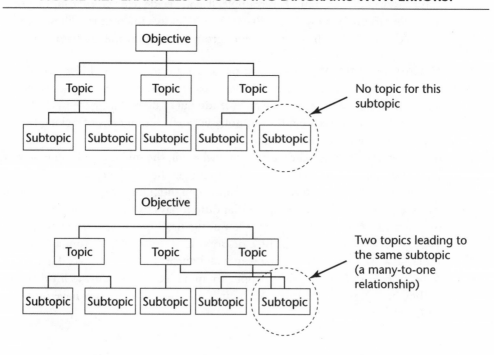

In many situations, it is not immediately clear which topics should form the top level of the diagram and which should be relegated to subtopic status. Your choice will make a difference in how you will proceed with the project. The topics you choose will drive the rest of your planning. They will be used to determine whom you will ask for help, how you organize the data collection, and, in many cases, how you organize your communications. Figure 4.3 shows two scoping diagrams for the same assignment. (These two examples are subsets of complete scoping diagrams. Other top-level topics might include customers and competition.) If you first divide the work into functional topics, you will probably develop a functional solution and may not focus sufficiently on customer requirements. If you divide the work into customer-focused topics, you may develop a more integrated solution for each, but you may miss some functional synergies.

FIGURE 4.3. TWO POSSIBLE SCOPING DIAGRAMS FOR A SINGLE ASSIGNMENT.

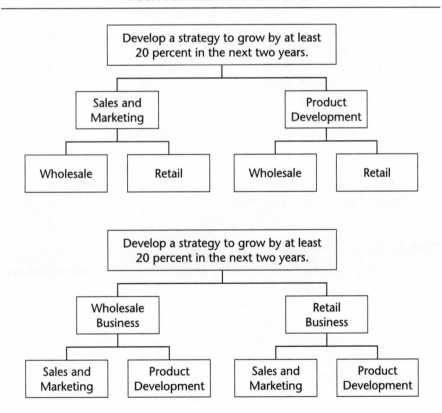

Mutually Exclusive and Collectively Exhaustive. Mutually exclusive and collectively exhaustive (MECE, pronounced "meecee") is an objective for the scoping diagram that is challenging to meet, and your diagram will be more helpful and compelling if you spend some time considering whether it is MECE. The topics at one level of the diagram are mutually exclusive if each is independent of the others. For example, in Figure 4.3, the top line of the second scoping diagram would not have been MECE if it had included "mass market" as an additional topic, because the mass market is served by the retail business. Topics are collectively exhaustive if together they completely cover the objective. When describing the businesses in Figure 4.3, you would not be collectively exhaustive if the strategy you are developing is intended to cover wholesale, retail, and distributors.

It is difficult to determine if topics on a scoping diagram are MECE. Your judgment is required to verify that you have all the topics you need to fully address the scope of the objective and whether some of them are superfluous. It may be useful to bear business school frameworks in mind when you test for completeness. For example, you may want to take into account product, price, promotion, and place if you are undertaking a marketing assignment, and you may choose to consider competitors, buyers, suppliers, new entrants, and substitutions as the top line of a strategy project. Table 4.3 provides other alternatives to help you test the top level for your project. However, do not be seduced into thinking that the top level of your diagram needs to be nothing more than the most appropriate framework. Your scoping diagram should reflect the specifics and idiosyncrasies of the situation you are facing. Very few clients will be impressed if you define their scope solely in terms of your favorite framework.

Be sure to use the client organization's words and definitions to describe the components of scope. In one organization, "development" might mean training, and in another, it might be a combination of training, mentoring, self-study, and experience.

Issue Trees

Some people prefer issue trees to scoping diagrams when structuring a project. An issue tree is similar to a scoping diagram in many ways. You begin with the objective of the assignment and develop a hierarchy that follows the scoping diagram rules. However, instead of topics and outputs, you create a hierarchy of anticipated recommendations. An issue tree that corresponds to the scoping diagram in Figure 4.1 appears in Figure 4.4.

The benefit of the issue tree approach is that it requires you to think about how to meet the objective from the outset. You start by thinking about the nature

TABLE 4.3. POSSIBLE FRAMEWORKS FOR ORGANIZING SCOPING DIAGRAMS.

Mnemonic	Definition	Relevant Types of Assignments
7S	Strategy, structure, systems, skills, style, staff, and shared values. There are seven, so this grouping nearly breaks the rules, but it can be categorized into hard Ss (strategy, structure, systems) and soft Ss (skills, style, staff, and shared values)	Process improvement Organizational design, development, and change
5 forces	Buyers, suppliers, new entrants, substitutes, and competition	Strategy
SWOT	Strengths, weaknesses, opportunities, threats	Strategy
4Ps	Product, price, promotion, and place	Marketing Strategy
3Cs	Customer, competition, company	Marketing Strategy
System Triangle	People, processes, and technology	Process improvement Organizational design, development, and change
Functions	Purchasing, manufacturing, sales, distribution, and administration	Various types of projects
Processes, value chain, business system	Order to delivery, raw materials to finished goods, product development; make, market, deliver	Process improvement Cost reduction
Geography, product lines, customer types, distribution channels		Various types of projects

Sources: For 7S: Waterman, R. H., Peters, T. J., and Philips, J. R. "Structure Is Not Organization." *Business Horizons*, 1980, *23*(3), 14–26. For 5 forces: Porter, M. *Competitive Strategy*. New York: Free Press, 1980.

of the solution rather than the situation the organization is facing. However, taking the extra step to think through topics and subtopics first is usually more expansive. It allows you to define the terrain of the project and then focus more specifically on each area. In addition, the scoping diagram is usually a more palatable product than an issue tree to share with your client and members of the client organization. A scoping diagram contains no specifics about the solution. An issue

FIGURE 4.4. ISSUE TREE.

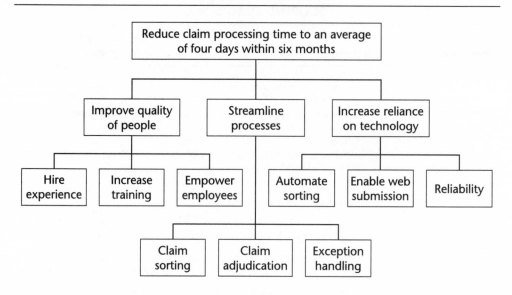

tree has the risk of encouraging people (including you) to think you already know the answer, which may cause you to fail to test your assumptions and to jump to conclusions without collecting sufficient data to justify them.

Summary

The scope of a project is defined by the constraints and conditions that limit it and by the scoping diagram that defines the boundaries of the objective. The topics in the scoping diagram describe all the areas that you will investigate in order to develop a solution. The deliverables or outputs describe the work products that you will produce as you conduct your investigation.

By working with your client to create a scoping diagram that meets the requirements of the project while taking into account your client's limitations, you can be assured that you and she will be in agreement about what your project is about, at least at the outset. Your ongoing challenge is to keep the scoping diagram firmly in the forefront of everyone's mind as you develop detailed plans for collecting the data.

Even with a scoping diagram to guide you, there are a great deal more data to collect and analyze than you will ever have time for. Chapter Five shows how to decide which data to collect to maximize the impact of your efforts.

CHAPTER FIVE

LESS IS MORE

Constructing Hypotheses

Just after my son Martin turned ten, he joined a neighborhood basketball team. The team practiced every Monday and Wednesday from 6:00 to 7:30 P.M. at the community center, about a five-minute walk from our house. During winter in Ohio, it is pitch dark by 5:30 P.M. I had to decide whether Martin was mature enough, and our neighborhood safe enough, for him to walk to and from practice by himself or if I would have to be his chaperone. I chose the former, but made sure that I was watching the clock on practice nights. If Martin wasn't home by 7:35 P.M., I took immediate action. What I did was informed by the hypotheses I had about where my son might be.

I didn't call the police, the hospitals, the airlines, or my mother. I first called the community center to see if the kids had already left. If they had, I called my next-door neighbor to see if Martin was there playing Nintendo with his friend Joe. Fortunately, I never had to go beyond those two phone calls.

This little vignette is an example of the problem-solving process at its most efficient. It is also an example of how most of us naturally conduct our daily lives. When we are faced with a choice about which data to collect to solve a problem or make a decision, we tend to hypothesize about what the right answer might be and then collect data to test that hypothesis. In my case, I hypothesized that Martin was still at the community center and checked that hypothesis by calling to see if I was right.

Notice that there is a big difference between assuming and hypothesizing. Assumptions cause all sorts of problems. If I had assumed he was at the community center, I might not have taken any action or might have gone to the center to get him. Had I been right, there wouldn't have been any adverse consequences, but had I been wrong, I would have lost valuable time finding out where he was, and my anxiety level would have shot up. Instead, I developed my best guess (my hypothesis) and then tested it. Had I not had a hypothesis, I would not have been able to decide if it would be more useful to call my mother or the community center.

The Value of Hypotheses

Hypothesizing is the most efficient way to structure data collection. Perhaps the biggest challenge associated with problem solving is deciding which data are important. As any problem solver or opportunity investigator knows, there are a lot more data than we will ever have time to collect. Too many data are just as troublesome as not enough data: in neither case is it possible to decide what to do. The sooner you can determine which data are relevant, the sooner you will reach conclusions and be able to design and implement your solutions. Hypotheses help order and limit data collection to those that will most likely prove to be useful.

Steve Keisling, an engineer by training, is a managing consultant for Landmark Graphics, a firm that helps petroleum exploration companies become more efficient and effective through the employment of appropriate information technologies. Steve believes that generating hypotheses and focusing data collection is the most challenging aspect of any assignment. "Quite possibly, the worst thing to do with an assignment is to run like hell, but down the wrong road." Hypotheses help Steve ensure that he is systematically collecting data that will make his recommendations supportable.

Hypotheses are not without drawbacks. By their very nature, they limit data collection. It is possible that you will miss a key piece of data entirely because you are looking in the wrong place. But without hypotheses, you are just as likely to miss something; there is more to choose from than you will ever have time to collect and absorb. Another drawback is the possibility that you will treat your hypotheses as the truth rather than conjectures to be tested. If you collect data that refute your hypotheses, you need to reconsider your hypotheses rather than doubt your data and keep collecting until you find the single fact that provides you the support you are looking for. In the case of Martin and the community center, even after being told that the children had left for the evening, I might have called back and asked the recreation administrator to check the washrooms or I might have gone over to see for myself. Although it's good to check your facts, I would have been wasting valuable time if Martin hadn't been there.

For hypotheses to be effective, you have to do the best you can at predicting what might be right and then be willing to accept that despite your efforts, you still might be wrong. Don't fall in love with your hypotheses, and don't beat yourself up if you develop some that are flawed. After all, a hypothesis is nothing more than an untested opinion.

Don't be nervous about developing hypotheses because you aren't sure of the right answer. That's the point. You do need to know something about the situation for your hypotheses to be helpful. You can generally get enough information from your client organization during preliminary meetings and interviews, from colleagues, and from Web and literature searches. You also have your own background and experience as a resource, whether it's from other projects, your relevant professional experience, or your education. If you spend anywhere from a few hours to a few days thinking about an organization and an industry, you should be able to develop some hypotheses about it. And remember that the more experience you have, the easier it is to develop hypotheses, but the greater risk is that you will treat your hypotheses as assumptions based on the strength of your convictions.

For example, when he was a junior consultant, Jeremy Raymond once faced a situation in which the partner in charge of a project was so stuck on his preconceived solution that it took too long for him to recognize what the client really needed. The client, the U.K. managing director of a Swiss pharmaceutical company, wanted to change the organization's corporate values. The partner believed, without much evidence except previous experience, that the answer lay in a greater focus on quality. Early interviews to understand the situation made it very clear to the team that partnership and innovation were much more important; product quality was already a core value. However, the partner persisted, and as Jeremy puts it, "The proposal bombed."

The scoping diagram should be used to bound the development of your hypotheses. For each subtopic, generate hypotheses that fully cover it while ensuring that none of them go outside its scope. The final list of hypotheses should include both those that you believe are highly probable and those that you aren't so sure about. Be sure to make choices when you select hypotheses. Don't hypothesize every possible reason for the decline in sales; rather, choose what you believe to be the primary reason.

Hypotheses are of two types: propositional and diagnostic.

Propositional Hypotheses

A propositional hypothesis is one that is easily tested, but the results may leave you asking the question, "So what?" For example, you might hypothesize that sales declined last year. It won't be very tough for you to find out whether you are correct, but the answer won't tell you what to do about it.

Here are some other examples of propositional hypotheses:

Advertising claims do not match product characteristics.
There is no difference in the marketing approach for the catalogue and the Web.
Department administration is time-consuming.

Even if you collect data and find that the hypotheses are correct, you are left wondering about the implications for the organization. In the case of the advertising claims, does this mean that customers have unmet expectations, that the organization could increase sales if it boasted more about its products, or that the marketing and product development departments don't communicate? In the second example, does the similarity in approaches result in a consistent message or a redundant channel? In the third, is the time well or poorly spent? By being specific and diagnostic, there is a greater probability that you will move your thinking forward when you determine whether you can accept the hypothesis.

Diagnostic Hypotheses

A diagnostic hypothesis, as the name implies, is one that diagnoses the situation. For example, you might hypothesize that sales declined because the organization's products are no longer cost competitive. It is much harder to determine if this hypothesis is true, but once you definitively identify the reason for the decline, you then have a clear direction for the project to take: do something about the cost position. If you find out that you are wrong, the data you have collected will undoubtedly point to other possibilities for the sales decline, such as product functionality or quality. You can then test these new hypotheses to determine what action to take. Diagnostic hypotheses often take the form of a fact and implication, or cause and effect.

Some diagnostic hypotheses aren't any more valuable than propositional hypotheses. For example, "Product complexity affects manufacturing throughput" suggests cause and effect, but lacks substance. It leaves you thinking, "How?" and "So what?"

It seems logical that complex products slow down throughput, but it would help to make that clear. In addition, because the relationship hypothesized is obvious, there is little that would be diagnosed as a consequence of finding this hypothesis to be true. It would be much more helpful to hypothesize about whether the high cost of manufacturing complex products is warranted by the return they generate.

The more specific a hypothesis is, the more valuable and often easier it is to test. For example, you could develop this hypothesis:

Competitive pressure is reducing sales volume.

However, this hypothesis gives no indication as to whether the competitive pressure is related to pricing, marketing, sales acumen, the number of competitors, product quality, product functionality, or any number of other factors. If you were faced with testing it, you would have to start down this list to see if any of these factors were the cause before you could establish whether to accept the hypothesis. It is much easier to test a hypothesis that guesses at the component of competitive pressure, such as the following one:

The competition's pricing tactics are reducing our sales volume.

Investigating only pricing rather than studying the entire marketing mix will test this hypothesis. There is the risk, of course, that you are wrong, in which case you would have to develop a new hypothesis. However, in collecting the data to test whether pricing tactics are the cause of sales volume reduction, you will develop insights into other better alternatives. The people you interview might tell you that the problem is packaging, or distribution, or an outstanding competitor product. What you learn during the investigation will ensure that your second hypothesis is far superior to your first.

Mike Griffiths once worked with a client to improve sales of a new product line. His team's first hypothesis was that poor customer service in the retail outlets was hampering new product sales. However, when they went to the store locations, they found that service was not the issue; rather, franchise owners were continuing to promote old product lines. Their revised hypothesis was that because the head office treated the franchise owners not as partners but as order takers, they had not found a way to motivate them to make the effort to learn about the new products. This second hypothesis proved to be correct. The team led a series of workshops between franchise owners and the head office directors to clarify the rationale for the new product line and jointly developed a compelling two-year plan.

You might wonder if it would have been just as productive to forget about developing hypotheses and head right to the stores to see what was going on. You would have gotten to the same place if you had done so in this case. However, in focusing on the stores, Mike and his team had already chosen not to investigate several alternative hypotheses. They had discarded the possibility that the new line was not what customers wanted and the suggestion that it was uncompetitive. They didn't investigate issues of supply and quality. Although their initial hypothesis was wrong, they saved a great deal of time by not looking into every prospect at the outset. Remember that initial hypotheses are not always wrong. In those cases where the first choice is the best choice, the time saved is enormous.

Questions

When employing the scientific method, you design an experiment to test your hypothesis. You carefully collect and record the data in the experimental and control conditions, ensuring that both are identical except for the variable you are testing. When testing hypotheses in a business environment, the level of control and the degree of proof possible are much less. Nevertheless, you do need to collect data to support or refute your position. The approach you use is more similar to a criminal investigation than to a scientific inquiry, however.

In a murder investigation, as we all know from television, the detectives look for evidence to determine who might have killed the victim. As quickly as possible, they develop a hypothesis or hypotheses about who might be responsible. To determine if their hypothesis is correct, they look for answers to at least the following questions:

- Is there a motive?
- Is there a means?
- Is there forensic evidence (fingerprints, for example, or evidence useful for DNA)?
- Are there witnesses?
- Did the accused have an opportunity?

Depending on the answers they get, they decide how to proceed. If there is clear forensic evidence, possibly nothing more is required. However, if there is a motive but no forensic evidence, no witnesses, and an airtight alibi, it becomes clear that the hypothesis should be rejected. Difficulties arise when the evidence is ambiguous. There is no forensic evidence and no witness, yet the suspect has no alibi and possesses a very clear motive. In this case, more digging is required.

Hypotheses in a problem-solving or opportunity development situation are tested in the same way. For each hypothesis, you develop a list of questions, the answers to which will provide sufficient evidence for you to accept or reject it. If a hypothesis requires more than seven (plus or minus two) questions to test it, it is probably too general or too complex. If a hypothesis requires only one question to test it, it is probably a propositional rather than a diagnostic hypothesis. Of course, this presumes that the question can be answered. If your hypothesis is that expanding the product line will increase sales, you could ask, "If we expand our product line, will sales increase?" It would be very hard to answer that question directly, short of expanding the product line and waiting to see what happens. You would have to answer several subquestions to make a judgment—for example:

- Do customers have unmet needs?
- Are customers interested in a sole supplier for all of their needs in this area?
- Could we be competitive if we expanded the product line?

In addition to avoiding questions that have no answer, you should avoid questions that have only one answer. For instance, there is no need to ask, "Should we improve profitability?"

Finally, you should avoid questions that take you outside the scope of the hypothesis and avoid hypotheses that take you outside the scope of the objective. You have to be constantly vigilant to ensure that you don't investigate areas that are not relevant or are only tangentially interesting. Do everything possible to avoid getting sidetracked: keep going back to the objective and scoping diagram to make sure you stay focused. All the benefits of hypotheses are lost if you fail to use them to drive data collection.

Let's work with the situation introduced earlier in this book: a health claims processing center would like to improve its throughput. Currently, the average time for a claim to be processed is six days from the time it reaches the processing center. A four-day turnaround would make the organization competitive with the industry leader. A project team has been created to see if they can improve throughput by 50 percent. They have created the scoping diagram we saw in Figure 4.1.

The team has also developed two hypotheses related to the topic of training:

A lack of training on specific contract features slows down claims adjudicators.

Training of newly hired employees would be more effective if it could be delivered as needed rather than all at once during their first days on the job.

Four questions would test the first hypothesis:

- What percentage of the time spent processing a claim is allocated to adjudication?
- How much time is devoted to looking up contract details as a percentage of total time worked?

- How much training would be required to keep up with changing contract details?
- What is the training retention rate for contract features?

If the answer to the first is "very little," you can immediately discard the hypothesis that training on contract features would improve throughput. However if the answer is "a lot," you need to delve into the other three questions.

The fourth question is a bit indirect. It implies that if people can't remember contract features after they've been trained extensively, there's no point in conducting the training. Another way to get at this issue might be to ask, "After training on contract features, how much time do adjudicators spend looking up contract details in comparison to the percentage of time before training?" Although this question is more precise, it might not get at the issue of degradation of memory over time. There is definitely an argument for including both questions. It would depend on how much evidence is required to convince both the hypothesizers and the client.

Asking a question such as, "What percentage of claims require the adjudicator to look up contract features?" would be superfluous because it's not the number of claims but how long they take to be processed that affects the overall objective. If a question requires judgment to answer, then it is not a good one. Asking, "Does a lack of training on specific contract features slow down claims adjudicators?" would be fruitless, since you could never find sufficient evidence to answer that question directly.

Asking, "Are contracts too complicated?" is an interesting and undoubtedly important point for the organization to consider, but it goes beyond the scope of this particular hypothesis. In fact, it may well be beyond the scope of the project. You should check with your client to see if she would be amenable to including product as a possible area for change.

Storyboards

Once you have developed hypotheses and questions, you are ready to start developing the final communication for the project. You begin to put this together before you have collected a single piece of data and before you have conducted a single interview. The storyboard's purpose is threefold:

- It helps you to determine if your hypotheses, when taken together, flow logically from one to the next and have the potential to create a coherent argument. In other words, it helps you establish whether you have a story to tell.
- It helps you to think about the kinds of data that your questions will elicit.

- It gives you a chance to think carefully about your sources: from whom and how you will collect the data and how challenging the data will be to obtain.

A storyboard consists of nothing more than mock-ups of the pages you might use to support your hypotheses. You begin by listing a hypothesis and the questions supporting it on a single frame, as shown in Figure 5.1.

Then you turn the questions into statements that would provide support for your hypothesis if they were true (Figure 5.2). The statement form provides another opportunity to check whether the questions are necessary and sufficient. Ultimately, your data may or may not support the statement you make. If they do not, it takes little effort to change them to tell the new story.

Finally, you create one or more frames showing how you will portray the data for each statement. For each frame, you list the data source, the data collection approach, the special data collection skills required, and how you will check

FIGURE 5.1. HYPOTHESIS AND SUPPORTING QUESTIONS.

Our competitor is cherry-picking our most profitable customers because of our inflexible stance on pricing.

- How does the average profitability of customers who have left in the past year compare to the profitability of our current customer base?
- Why have customers left?
- How does our price vary by customer segment?
- How do our competitors price?

FIGURE 5.2. HYPOTHESIS AND SUPPORTING STATEMENTS.

Our competitor is cherry-picking our most profitable customers because of our inflexible stance on pricing.

- The average profitability of customers who leave is x percent higher than those who stay.
- Former customers left because they could get better pricing elsewhere.
- Customers who require little customer support pay the same for our product as those who require a great deal of support.
- Several of our competitors provide a low-cost product with no customer service.

the accuracy of the data. Figure 5.3 provides an example for the statements in
Figure 5.2.

At each stage, you check to make sure that the story makes sense. When
the questions are turned into statements, you verify that the statements fully support
the hypothesis—that anyone reading them would come to the same conclusion.
Obviously, if you find gaps or redundancies, you fix them. For example,

FIGURE 5.3. FRAMES FOR STATEMENTS IN FIGURE 5.2.

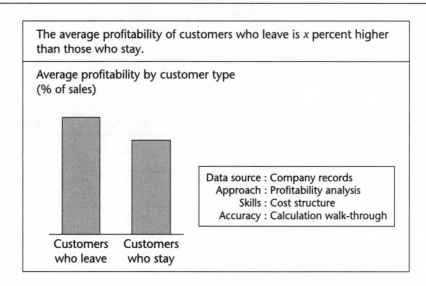

The average profitability of customers who leave is x percent higher
than those who stay.

Average profitability by customer type
(% of sales)

Customers   Customers
who leave   who stay

Data source : Company records
Approach : Profitability analysis
Skills : Cost structure
Accuracy : Calculation walk-through

Former customers left because they could get better pricing elsewhere.

- The HR manager at JF Controls said he didn't want to pay Cadillac
  prices since his employees only have Chevrolet needs.
- Jones Manufacturing moved to Smith because of pricing.
- Jackson Products requested proposals from six processors. We were
  the most expensive.

Data source: Former customers
Approach: Interviews
Skills: Finding interviewees
Accuracy: Range of customers

FIGURE 5.3. FRAMES FOR STATEMENTS IN FIGURE 5.2. (*Continued*)

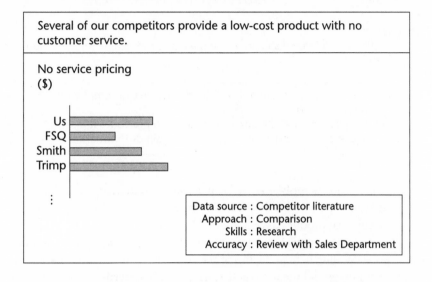

Several of our competitors provide a low-cost product with no customer service.

No service pricing
($)

Us
FSQ
Smith
Trimp

⋮

Data source : Competitor literature
Approach : Comparison
Skills : Research
Accuracy : Review with Sales Department

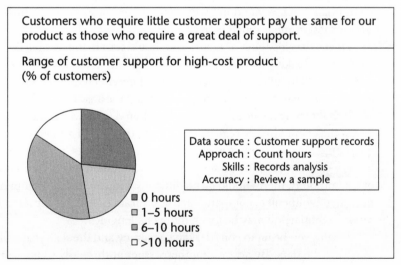

Customers who require little customer support pay the same for our product as those who require a great deal of support.

Range of customer support for high-cost product
(% of customers)

Data source : Customer support records
Approach : Count hours
Skills : Records analysis
Accuracy : Review a sample

■ 0 hours
□ 1–5 hours
■ 6–10 hours
□ >10 hours

in Figure 5.4, the statements do not fully support the hypothesis that Supplies Unlimited should develop a new product line: there is no evidence that the firm would be capable of developing sufficiently unique or low-cost products to compete in this market. You have the choice of narrowing your hypothesis to something that states that current products and pricing are not competitive

FIGURE 5.4. SUPPORTING STATEMENTS THAT DO NOT FULLY SUPPORT THE HYPOTHESIS.

> Supplies Unlimited should develop a new product line for the school supply market.
>
> ---
>
> - Current products are not sufficiently unique to exempt them from aggressive pricing action.
> - Supplies Unlimited's current cost position precludes it from taking the aggressive pricing action necessary to gain distribution.

in the school supply market or of adding a statement that indicates evidence of the required capabilities, for example, "Supplies Unlimited has a long history of effective product development."

When you create the frames portraying the data, confirm that the frame supports the statement at the top of the page. In Figure 5.5, the chart in the first frame does not give all the information necessary to determine whether aggressive pricing is possible since you don't have competitor prices against which to compare. The second frame is much better.

As you develop the storyboard, you should start to think about the source of the data you are looking for and how difficult they will be to collect. For example, if your question is, "Do different segments prefer different channels?" it will be necessary to undertake market segmentation work to find the answer. This will involve market research that may include focus groups and surveys, as well as customer interviews, unless the client already regularly conducts this sort of research. In contrast, the question, "How do our prices compare with the those of the competition?" could be very easy or very difficult to answer. If your client sells a comparable product or a commodity, there should be no difficulty. However, if the company sells something that is difficult to compare, such as insurance, or if pricing includes customer service, comparison may be much more challenging.

Finally, you begin to consider data accuracy and the skills that will be required to collect the data. By addressing these issues at this early stage, you can be sure that you match the capabilities of your team with the skills required.

Although it is highly unlikely that the storyboard you put together will become the final presentation, its discipline enables you to understand how much work will be required to collect the data that will allow you to answer the questions you have posed. Furthermore, the exercise assists in determining whether the people you ask to help you collect the data are absolutely clear about what you are looking for. It is much easier for someone to complete a blank chart than to imagine what

FIGURE 5.5. SUPPORT FOR THE STATEMENTS.

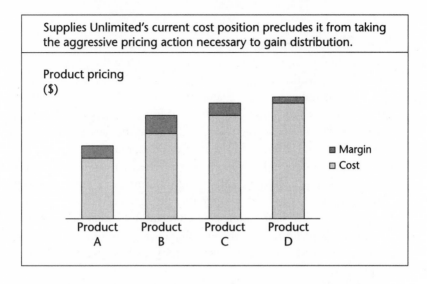

Supplies Unlimited's current cost position precludes it from taking the aggressive pricing action necessary to gain distribution.

Product pricing ($)

Margin
Cost

Product A   Product B   Product C   Product D

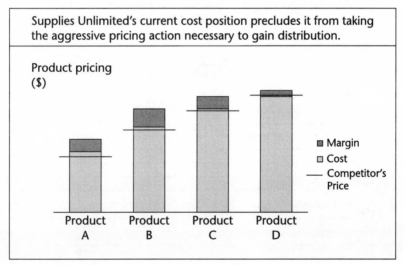

Supplies Unlimited's current cost position precludes it from taking the aggressive pricing action necessary to gain distribution.

Product pricing ($)

Margin
Cost
—— Competitor's Price

Product A   Product B   Product C   Product D

you mean when you ask them to find the answer to a question such as: "What is Supplies Unlimited's cost position?"

Paul Lucas believes that "to have any hope of getting anything done requires process." He insists on storyboards because he finds that their discipline helps keep the entire problem-solving process under control. If you can't write it down, you don't know what you know or even if you know anything.

The Data Matrix

The storyboard provides insight into the sources of data required for initial hypotheses. Combining this information into a data matrix is the first step in estimating the time it is likely to take to complete the project. By organizing all your data collection needs in one place, you can minimize the number of times you have to call on or investigate each source. Without a data matrix, there is a much greater chance that you will forget to ask someone for a key piece of information and either have to go back and request the data again or proceed without them. Figure 5.6 shows the format of the data matrix.

The data matrix has rows listing all the hypotheses and questions for the assignment, and columns containing the sources of data identified in the storyboard. In the matrix itself, you identify the data collection approach you plan to employ. By seeing your data collection techniques all at once, you can determine if you are focusing excessively on a single way to obtain information. Be wary of using your favorite approach because it's your favorite, not because it's the most appropriate.

Reading vertically, the data matrix shows all the questions that you will use each source to answer. This enables you to develop a data collection instrument

FIGURE 5.6. DATA MATRIX.

		Sources of Data						
		Managing Director	General Manager	Head of IT	Customers	Administrative Staff	Trainers	Records/ Documents
Hypo 1	Q1					I		D
	Q2		I			I		D
	Q3			I	S	MR		D
Hypo 2	Q1					I		MR
	Q2				S		I	
	Q3	I	I		S		I	D
	Q4						O	D
Hypo 3	Q1					MR		
	Q2		I			I		
	Q3		I			I		
	Q4					I		MR
Hypo 4	Q1		I					
	Q2	I						
	Q3							

Note: I = interview; O = observation; D = document search; S = survey; MR = management reports.

for each source with greater confidence that it will be complete. You can also assess whether you are relying disproportionately on a single source (which may be the case with the general manager or administrative staff in Figure 5.6) or not using a source to its fullest potential (the IT manager).

Reading horizontally enables you to ensure that you have enough sources to assume data validity but not so many that you collect more data than you need. If, after completing the matrix, you realize that you are going to only a single source to answer a question such as Hypothesis 4, Question 2 in Figure 5.6, you can ask yourself if this approach will be sufficient to ensure validity or if you ought to check with another source as well. In contrast, Hypothesis 2, Question 3 has five sources. Perhaps this is more than you need to answer the question.

The data matrix enables you to see the entirety of your data collection plan and determine its appropriateness in an integrated rather than a piecemeal fashion. You use the matrix to test it for both efficiency and effectiveness by asking three questions:

- Are you demonstrating creativity in your data gathering, or are you using predominantly the same technique and the same source?
- Is your data collection plan cost conscious? Are you using too many sources to answer a particular question?
- Is your plan complete? Are you using enough sources to check the validity of the data you gather?

With a completed data matrix, the project work plan becomes much easier to construct.

Summary

Data collection forms the core of most problem-solving and opportunity assessment projects. It is easy to show what you have accomplished and is therefore a very satisfying activity. It is also seductive. There are many more data about any problem or opportunity than you will ever have time to collect, but it often seems that the situation will be completely elucidated if you just collect a little bit more. Hypotheses enable you to order and limit your data collection to that which is most likely to be important and useful. Rather than becoming mired in the seduction of what more data may promise, you plan which data you will need in advance and modify your plan only as you learn about the situation through testing your hypotheses. As a close colleague has often reminded me, "You can always get more data, but you can never put them back." Gathering too much data is an irrecoverable expense.

Quality in hypotheses can be elusive. A hypothesis must relate to the scope of the assignment, and it must be testable. If it is not clear and concise, it will be harder to test.

The storyboard helps to clarify your data collection intentions and enables you to determine in advance whether your plan will result in a logical story to help your client meet his objective.

Finally, the data matrix provides a mechanism that will illustrate the completeness and appropriateness of your data collection plan.

Together, hypotheses, questions, storyboards, and data matrices help you maintain discipline and thought leadership. They provide you with an efficient and logical way to explore the problems or opportunities facing your client. Now you are ready to develop a project plan that will truly reflect what needs to be done.

CHAPTER SIX

HOW, WHEN, AND WHO?

Planning the Effort

Most organizations have project management methodologies. There is no point in reinventing the wheel. If one exists, use it. If one doesn't exist, use technology such as Microsoft Project to help you. But don't fall prey to thinking that the plan is a good one if it's automated. A plan is only as good as the thinking behind it. Remember that any plan is better than no plan, and a complete plan will work—if you execute effectively.

This chapter provides an overview and discussion of how to connect the planning tools and techniques used in organizations to the rest of the problem-solving process. More important, it explains how to connect the plan to the client and the organization for which it is being developed.

A complete plan requires you to determine *what* you are going to do, *how* you should do it, *who* should be involved, and *when* and *where* activities should happen.

Answering *what* begins with the project's objective. Scoping the project, developing hypotheses and questions, and creating a data matrix follow. The data matrix provides a list of all the activities that need to be accomplished to collect the data that will help you solve the problem or capitalize on the opportunity. With it in hand, you can determine the best way to collect the data.

Your judgment and experience are now required to answer the following questions:

- How risky is the project?
- How should it be organized?
  How many phases should there be?
  How many levels are optimal?
  What constitutes a piece of work small enough to be manageable?
- How many people will be needed, and what skills should they have?
- What is a logical task sequence?
- How long will the project take?
- What budget will be required?

Of course, the larger the project is, the more challenging it will be to manage. But how much management and control are required? If you are working with people who have lots of experience with the kind of work that the project entails, management may mean no more than agreeing on who does what and moving forward. If there are junior people who have not engaged in this sort of project before, they may need more guidance.

How Risky Is the Project?

The fundamental reason for planning a project is to assess its risk so that you can take proactive steps to prevent a potential problem from occurring and make preliminary plans to react should a potential risk transpire. There are six types of risk to consider in any project, as outlined in Table 6.1.

To determine the consequences of a potential risk, you should develop scenarios to determine what might happen should a potential problem arise. For example, if you find you have to increase resources, what is the impact on the cost of the project? Is there any room to manage the project's quality if you don't have as much to spend on it as you had hoped? If you are faced with a shortage in staff support, should you allow costs to increase by hiring contractors, should you reduce the scope of the effort, or should you extend the project deadline? You need to determine which of these undesirable alternatives is the least, as well as the most, acceptable.

By beginning with the premise that risk is the fundamental driver of any project, you keep risk firmly in the forefront as you make choices about your plan. You need to assess its probability and the probable impact of each risk you identify. You can't deal with every possibility, so focus first on the most likely risks with the highest

TABLE 6.1. SIX TYPES OF RISK IN A PROJECT.

Type of Risk	Example
Time	You may not meet the schedule.
Cost	The project may cost more than anticipated. The ongoing costs after implementation may be too high.
Quality	The solution may not fit the organization. The solution may not be good enough to meet the objective.
Resources	People needed for the project may not be available. People assigned to the project may not have the necessary skills.
Scope	The environment may change. The objectives of the project may change.
Size	The bigger the project, the greater the chance is that something will go wrong. The larger the team, the more significant the chance is that the project will take longer in terms of actual time.
Confidence	The less confidence, the less likely successful implementation is but too much confidence may result in being blindsided.

TABLE 6.2. RISK ASSESSMENT MATRIX.

Risk	Probability	Impact	Action
Data unavailable	High	Medium	Estimate with a sample if risk transpires
Jack gets called off project	Low	High	Escalate with senior management now

negative impact. Then think through the trade-offs, and be clear about the most appropriate decisions to make should the project go off the rails. Finally, decide whether to incorporate proactive risk reduction strategies into your plan or to presume, given your probability assessment, that disaster won't strike. Table 6.2 provides an example of how to set out this information.

How Should the Project Be Organized?

The number of phases within the project is determined by the need for closure. The end of a phase usually indicates that you are finished and do not plan to revisit what you have already accomplished. In traditional consulting projects, the end of a phase is usually a time to decide whether to continue, whether to use the same team, and whether to use the same consulting firm.

The number of levels is determined according to the size and subsequent manageability of each component. What is manageable varies from one person or team to another. Depending on skill level and motivation, some people are comfortable with a piece of work that takes weeks to complete, while others need support and closure at the end of every day. The people who should be involved in this planning are those who are best able to estimate the capabilities of the people involved, as well as accurately assess the nature of the job. It often helps to ask the people who will be responsible for completing the work what effort they think it will require. But don't ask them unless you intend to listen to their responses. It's demeaning to ask someone how long something will take and then tell that person that his or her estimate is unacceptable.

A work breakdown structure is a clear and visual way to help you keep track of how you have organized the work. As you can see in Figure 6.1, it looks a lot like a scoping diagram or an organization chart. It defines the pieces of work in a project and roughly orders them from left to right.

A work breakdown structure is an activity-based hierarchy. The bottom level is a work element whose completion can be measured and whose quality can be

FIGURE 6.1. WORK BREAKDOWN TEMPLATE.

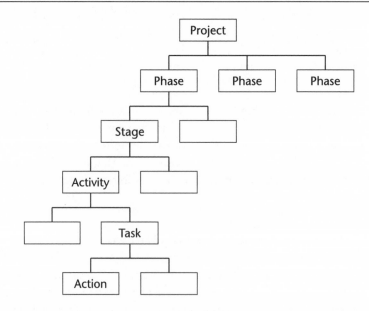

evaluated. For example, completing the data collection for a frame in a storyboard might be a work element in one project. In another, a set of interviews might be one element, the analysis of those interviews might be a second, and the completion of the storyboard frame might be a third. Work elements sum up to higher-level tasks, activities, stages, and phases. The effort represented by a task is the sum of the effort that is represented by all the work elements that feed into that task. Similarly, the effort represented by an activity is the sum of all the effort represented by the tasks that feed into it.

It is important to recognize that a work breakdown structure and a scoping diagram are not the same thing, and they do not serve the same purpose. A scoping diagram lays out what needs to be investigated; a work breakdown structure lays out how it needs to be accomplished. The content of the boxes in a scoping diagram comprises the topics to be covered; the content of the boxes in a work breakdown structure lays out the work to be completed.

A work breakdown structure can be developed top down or bottom up, or by beginning with a template from a project that has been successfully completed. If you begin with a template, your task is to determine how this project will differ from the previous one. A bottom-up approach requires that you list all the possible work elements that must be completed during this project and then organize them into tasks, activities, stages, and phases. The data matrix is the source of the work elements.

Top-down work planning begins with the major work units and then breaks them down until each piece of work is a manageable work element. The data matrix is used in this case to verify completeness.

The task of breaking down a project into pieces should be done in conjunction with both the people who will be responsible for completing the work elements and with the client. How often does the client want to be informed of progress? What work products is she interested in seeing? How can and should value and progress be demonstrated? Not all clients will be able to answer these questions at the start of the project, although those with solid project experience probably will. If your client doesn't know the answers yet, you can use this as an opportunity to help her become a better overseer of the project by explaining your thinking process.

What you call each of the levels is entirely dependent on the norms of the organization in which you are working. Using the language of Figure 6.1, *action* is the place where work gets done. It is the equivalent of a work element in this nomenclature. All of the rest of the boxes summarize the actions. The rules you follow to create a work breakdown structure are the same as those for a scoping diagram: seven plus or minus two, horizontal and vertical logic, and, as much as possible, mutually exclusive and collectively exhaustive.

Figure 6.2 shows a sample work breakdown structure. The project it describes has four activities: assess the current situation, develop alternatives, evaluate and select, and, finally, implement.

In the example work breakdown structure in Figure 6.2, only *create and conduct selection process* shows the specific work elements to be completed. *Assess current situation* is broken down to the task level. Whether this is appropriate depends on the people who are assigned to each activity.

Why is it worthwhile to begin the planning of a project with a work breakdown rather than solely with a sequencing of all the tasks? The work breakdown enables you to chunk the work and is much easier to follow than a long list of items to do. Nevertheless, the work breakdown structure does not describe the sequence

FIGURE 6.2. EXAMPLE WORK BREAKDOWN STRUCTURE.

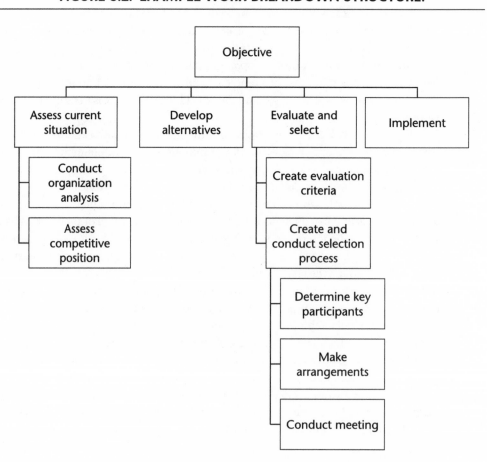

of tasks in detail, so you must still understand which activities require others to be complete before they can be started.

In the example in Figure 6.2, *assess current situation* must be completed before the other activities can begin. The next two activities can begin in parallel, but the selection process cannot be completed until *develop alternatives* is done. Finally, it is not possible to begin implementation until *evaluate and select* is finished.

How Many People and What Skills?

It may be helpful to create a skills inventory of the people who may be involved in the project before you decide who does what. A skills inventory will help you determine if the team composition and size are appropriate for the project defined by the data matrix and the work breakdown. It will also help you make the right assignments and will indicate who might be able to replace or assist an overloaded resource. The skills that are important to keep track of depend on the project. Remember that project skills such as communication and team management are just as important as analytical skills.

Assessing skills and choosing team members is a luxury on many projects. Often the people who are assigned to a team are selected based on availability or political necessity, not on skills and aptitude. But even in this case, it is worth exploring their capabilities. A lack of appropriate skills can be managed; a lack of knowledge cannot.

The sample skills inventory in Table 6.3 provides considerable insight into potential issues on this project. At 100 percent commitment and with needed skills, both Jacquelyn and Mark ought to be productive team members. Unless she is there to learn, Kate won't be very helpful. Nick has the right skill set but not enough time. You might want to negotiate with him to see if you can get more of it. Unless he has knowledge that cannot be duplicated as well as great discipline,

TABLE 6.3. SKILLS INVENTORY.

Team member	Time Availability	Interviewing	Process Knowledge	Information Technology
Nick	20 percent	X	X	X
Jacquelyn	100 percent	X	X	
Kate	50 percent			
Mark	100 percent			X
Julian	10 percent		X	

Julian will also be a problem: 10 percent of someone's time is about half a day a week. If you can get that time in a concentrated chunk, it might be helpful, but typically what happens is that people who devote 10 percent of their time or less to a project are very costly to the team in terms of the time required to update them every time they join in. They may do nothing more than attend meetings. If that's helpful, don't worry about it, but if you expect someone to contribute work products, you will need more of their time to ensure that they will be able to deliver.

What Task Sequence?

The amount of effort you put into sequencing and organizing tasks depends on the complexity of the project. You may be able to manage the entire effort in a simple spreadsheet, or you may want to use planning software to help you. If you do the latter, you will want to develop a Gantt or a PERT chart to help you with sequence.[1]

Table 6.4 illustrates a starting point for the work plan for a simple project. Whether you list activities, tasks, or work elements depends on the detail the team requires. In this case, the pieces of work are at a fairly high level, indicating that this is an experienced team. Under "Dependencies," you list what must be complete before this work element can be started. "Issues" are potential areas

TABLE 6.4. WORK PLAN.

Work Element	Dependencies	Issues	End Products	Responsibility	Timing
Define needs		Depth of analysis	Needs assessment	Mary	Two weeks
Develop request for proposal (RFP)	Define needs	Level of detail	RFP	Jack and Mary	Two weeks
Develop selection process	Define needs	Baseline qualifications, criteria	Selection process	Serena	One week
Select vendor	Develop selection process; develop RFP	Who should be involved	Decision	All	Two weeks

for concern or details that have not yet been sorted out. "End Products," "Responsibility," and "Timing" are self-explanatory.

How Long Will the Project Take?

One of the great challenges of any planning effort is determining how long the project will take. Here are a few guidelines:

• *Don't try to hit a moving target.* If you aren't sure exactly what the project entails, don't estimate it. Hold off until you have a data matrix, a work breakdown, and a sense of the people who will be involved.

• *Try to find a reference or metric against which to compare.* If you've done this sort of project before, use what happened last time as a benchmark. If you haven't, ask someone who has how much time they spent. Keep track of your own estimates as well as the time that activities actually took. You can use this information for future estimates and also to understand your own estimation tendencies. If, in general, you find that activities take longer than you anticipate, try to add this extra time to your estimate.

• *Break work down into small enough pieces.* It is much easier to estimate a small piece of work than a large one. If you don't know how long it will take to prepare for and conduct twenty interviews, for example, extrapolate from how long one would take. If you don't know how long it will take to assess the current situation, break the activity down into the departments you will investigate, the people to whom you will speak, the other research you will undertake, and so forth. Each of these elements should be easier to estimate individually.

• *Ask people who will do the work for their estimate.* It is usually easier to estimate how long it will take you to do something than how long it will take someone else. Ask others for their individual estimates, and then listen to their answers carefully. What might take one person a week to accomplish may take another a day and a half.

• *Don't forget about the difference between actual time and elapsed time.* Elapsed time is typically 20 to 40 percent longer than actual time. In the average eight-hour day, most people work only five hours. There are other considerations as well—for example:

People you need to interview, equipment, and data may not be available when you need them. Try to accommodate this reality into your plan by asking early and by inserting other tasks that aren't dependent on these resources. Recognize that sometimes you will simply have to wait.

People on the team may have other duties that get in the way of the time they have committed to the project. Their priorities may also change.

For people who are not working on the project full time, it will take a while for them to ramp up and become current again each time they come back to the project.

Personal issues compromise the available time. People get sick and take vacations.

The trouble with estimating project time carefully is that the amount of time available is usually less than the amount of time you need. There are only a few ways to legitimately shorten elapsed time for a project:

• *Increase resources.* This works only if the tasks can be split efficiently. Every time you add someone to a project, interactions and interpretations increase exponentially. With three people on a project, there are three lines of communication. With four people, there are six, and with five there are ten.

• *Rearrange the order of activities to make use of the slack time associated with waiting for equipment, people, or data.*

• *Reduce the amount of work.* For example, do you really need to conduct all the interviews you have planned?

• *Control slack time.* If you ask someone how long something will take, he may well tell you time that includes some slack just to be sure that he finishes before the deadline. Most people who are given a deadline procrastinate until the last possible minute to begin. And if something goes wrong, they will run out of time. When you multiply this behavior by all the people involved in the project, you quickly realize that the project will probably take longer than it needs to and you won't have any reserve if something really does go wrong. The remedy is hard to implement, however. You need to convince people to give you an honest estimate of the time their piece of the project will take and then assure them that if something goes wrong, you will give them more time. Of course, you have to build slack into the overall project to ensure that you have time to give.

• *Renegotiate the definition of the project.* This requires changing the scope and possibly the objective as well. If you reduce the length of your project without making one or more of these types of changes, you will meet your schedule only if you work longer hours. Unfortunately, longer hours, particularly over time, have a diminishing return. If you have worked eighty hours a week for one week you may be productive fifty of those hours. If you work eighty hours for ten weeks, you may find that you are productive only thirty-five of them.

What Budget Will Be Required?

Once you know how long each resource will be required, you can estimate the project budget. Again, you will often find that the initial estimated budget is too high. Remedies are few, and very similar to those suggested for reducing time. Doing less is the obvious first way to cut a budget. You can also use less expensive resources. Here, however, you need to make the trade-off between how fast and effectively more and less expensive resources work. Your challenge is to determine the best choice given your objectives and constraints.

I worked with a woman a few years ago who was responsible for the systems integration of a bank acquisition. As soon as she was made responsible, Cheryl (a pseudonym) realized that the project was in serious trouble. It did not seem possible to end up with a well-working set of systems on time and within budget. She hadn't done a bad job; she had been assigned to a project that couldn't meet all its goals.

The project could be completed, but not within the time constraints placed on it. And it was conceivable that it could be finished within budget, but that approach would also take much longer than the time available. Time pressure was enormous because every month that the project was delayed would cost the bank $1.4 million, as it would have to keep the acquired bank's data center open to process its transactions. Since time was of the essence, Cheryl had to decide where to cut in terms of functionality and how much of a budget overrun would be tolerable. As is often the case, the original budget was set when very little information was available about what was involved in completing the integration.

Cheryl overspent her budget by $3 million to get the job done because she realized that those expenditures would quickly be dwarfed by the reduced operating costs after the integration was complete. She also cut functionality but did not reduce the quality of the systems that were installed. The choices were hard, and many people criticized her in the short term, but she could easily justify her decisions.

Summary

Planning a project is a case of using a disciplined approach to sort through what needs to happen, who is best suited to do it, how long it should take, and how much it should cost. Such an effort rarely occurs in a linear fashion. An initial plan may turn out to require much more time and cost much more than is practical for the problem being solved. You may find that you don't have the right resources, and they won't become available. When that happens, you change the plan, going back as far as necessary, perhaps even to the objective, in order to get the project matched as much as possible to the constraints of the situation and the outcomes the client wants.

Flexibility is key to successful planning. Once you have developed a project plan, use it to see how you are doing, but don't be afraid to change it as circumstances change and your understanding of the situation improves. Flexibility isn't all that's important, however. You also need to nurture the commitment of everyone involved.

CHAPTER SEVEN

PEOPLE HAVE TO BE PART OF IT

Nurturing Commitment

When you suggest that your client should take action to change a situation, you are encouraging her to embark on an effort fraught with challenge, frustration, and risk. No matter how appropriate your advice is, both you and she will face resistance and second-guessing. No matter how carefully you have presold your suggestions, people will suddenly see all sorts of flaws that had never occurred to them before.

People dislike change for its own sake. They don't like it even if it's critical to the survival of the organization. It's not fun, and it takes effort. They find comfort in the familiar. They offer a litany of excuses. We've all heard these:

"This is wrong for this organization right now."

"I'm doing all I can."

"Fix the other problem first."

"Give me more people, budget, time, . . ."

"It's not really a problem."

"We've tried that. It won't work here."

"I don't have control."

Sometimes those who are the least vocal are the most resistant to change. Some people think if they just lay low, the whole idea will disappear. What they say may or may not be related to the real reason for their resistance:

- *Fear.* If they perceive that the solution will threaten their power, status, relationships, or control, they aren't likely to be in favor of it.
- *Lack of understanding.* When they don't know what to do, don't know why they should do it, or don't know how, they are likely to be far less cooperative.
- *Lack of faith in the people promoting the solution.*
- *Experience with the organization's history of failed initiatives.*
- *A belief that things are moving too quickly, or that they think they are already facing too much stress and don't believe they can cope with more.*
- *Unmet expectations.* Regardless of how unrealistic their hopes were, if the solution is not as good as people hoped it would be, they are likely to resist.

There are also legitimate reasons for people to resist. If the solution is not a good one in their eyes, their intellectual honesty will compel them to resist. If the solution will hinder some people while helping others, those hindered have a legitimate reason to resist. Finally, people resist when they're faced with a lot of effort, and often they are. What's a problem solver to do?

This chapter describes a frame of mind that makes change and implementation much easier. But you have to start at the beginning of the project, not after you've designed the solution.

Essentials for Success

Successful solutions are the result of careful planning and execution throughout the entire assignment.[1] For solutions to be successful, they need the following foundations:

- The project must be defined in terms of specific client results to be achieved, not the problem solver's expertise or products.
- The project scope must be determined by the client's readiness for change rather than the problem to be solved.
- The project must aim for incremental successes rather than one big solution.
- There must be a close partnership between the client and the problem solver throughout the entire assignment.

The notion of incremental successes rather than a big solution is often difficult for people to accept. It may seem like a waste of time to fix something small, only to have to refix it when the next element of the solution is put into place. However, in most situations, it is the only viable approach.

Nevertheless, sometimes an incremental solution just won't do it. For example, in 1967, Sweden changed from driving on the left side of the road to driving on the right. An incremental change might have had the trucks change on the first day.

Participation Is Key

Real and broad-based participation is key to the successful design and implementation of solutions. David Cooperrider, a colleague of mine at the Weatherhead School of Management, believes so strongly in the value of involvement that he organizes summits of up to one thousand people to discuss together how an organization should move forward.

At Roadway Express, summit involvement includes unionized dockworkers, truck drivers, and mechanics, as well as clerks, supervisors, managers, vice presidents, and the president. Roadway's union is the International Brotherhood of Teamsters, so excuses about how hard it is to get people to work together don't wash. There are no alternatives.

Niels Dechow, another Weatherhead colleague, believes that "the most challenging aspect of getting people involved is making them feel comfortable enough with you to be open enough to tell you what you need to know to understand the situation fully." Deciding whether to engage often happens as a consequence of how you react to their initial attempts. As always, actions speak louder than words. Responding directly works much better than stating that you'll be friends for the next three months or socializing by decree. You can't tell adults to "play nice."

Beware of Filtering Communications

We all use filters when communicating with others.[2] We consciously and unconsciously decide what we will share and how we will share it, what we will hear and how we will hear it. Our filters distort our actions and reactions, as do those of the people with whom we are communicating.

Most people employ at least the following filters:

- *Self-image.* How sure you are of yourself and how expert you believe you are will affect how assertive you are. You are more likely to get defensive when someone challenges your position if you believe you are an expert than if you are unsure of your contribution.
- *Image of others.* How much confidence you have in the other person's expertise and power will affect how you listen to him. There is a big difference between listening for someone else's contributions and listening to see if that person understands your position. If you perceive the other person as having higher

status than you do, you may divert your attention away from the content of the discussion to focus more on its relationship aspects.

• *Definition of the situation.* If all the participants in a communication do not have the same definition of the situation, including purpose, roles, politics, norms, and values, there may be very little communication at all. It is important to clarify the situation before the communication goes off the rails.

• *Motives, feelings, intentions, and attitudes.* If you are trying to gain agreement for an idea, you communicate much differently than if you are trying to understand someone's position on an issue. Your motives, intentions, feelings, and attitudes drive what you will ask, what someone will answer, and what you will hear.

• *Expectations.* Depending on whether you expect someone to be receptive or critical, slow or quick to understand, you may say and hear very different things. If you expect agreement, you may not hear disagreement. If you expect a logical argument, you may not test to be sure that it is logical—at least not during the communication.

One consequence of these filters is that you must work very hard to be conservative in your belief that you understand others and liberal in your effort to learn from and about them.

Another consequence is that the opinions of the people in the client organization about the facts are just as important as yours, and they are unlikely to be the same, as illustrated in Figure 7.1. The vertical axis portrays the problem-solving team's beliefs, and the horizontal axis, the client's.

Three rules that are exceedingly difficult to follow (and rules 2 and 3 are just variations of rule 1) may help you to stay open to others:

Rule 1: Treat everyone the way you would like to be treated, but remember that everyone is not like you.

Do you want to be manipulated? Do you like it when someone tries to convince you of something that you are sure is a dumb idea? Do you feel good when someone ignores your point of view? Do you believe him when someone says he knows exactly how you feel or what you're thinking or what you need? Neither does anyone else.

Rule 2: Assume that other people are as clever as you are.

How often are you tricked into changing your mind, so that your mind stays changed? Have you ever told someone you agreed with her just to get her out of your office? Do you believe people when they tell you, "This is just what you need"? Can you tell when someone is not open and forthright? Most people answer these questions the same way as you do.

Rule 3: Start from their point of view, not yours.

Are you convinced when someone tells you her idea is fantastic, good for the organization, or important . . . ? Do you like being told you're wrong, even when it takes many more words?

The point of the rules is easy to see. It's the execution that's challenging.

Motivation Is Elusive

Many of the problems associated with implementing new ideas in organizations stem from making superficial assumptions about how people think and act:[3]

- If you think that people act in their own self-interest, you may also think that all you have to do is demonstrate to them that making whatever change proposed is in their own self-interest. It also helps to provide concrete incentives.

FIGURE 7.1. DIVERGENT OPINIONS OF THE PROBLEM-SOLVING TEAM AND THE CLIENT ORGANIZATION.

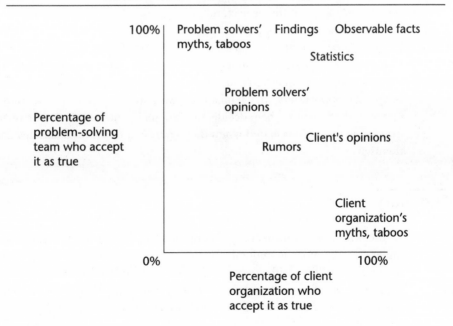

- If you think that people act in imitation of those around them or because they have a high need for affiliation, you may think you have to provide role models or champions that have sufficient credibility to be able to encourage others to follow their lead.
- If you think that people act in obedience, that they are compliant and do what they are told, all you need to do is exercise your power and authority.

The reality, of course, is that people have many motivations, and different people have different motivations at different times. It isn't possible to uncover them all. What motivates one person repulses another. If you try to maneuver people to your way of thinking, you are bound to fail.

Convincing people to change the way they do things means convincing them to make many, many small decisions in the way that you would like them to. It's not like asking them to buy a product or vote for a candidate once. While appealing through sales tactics or coercion may seem to work in the short term, people are unlikely to support the solution over the long haul unless they decide for themselves that the change makes sense.

To make change work and last, it is important to give people a real opportunity to participate and contribute. Rather than convincing them to agree with the solution, you have to give them an opportunity to choose to agree. This requires you to advocate your position, but at the same time to give people a chance to ask questions, raise issues, and test your logic for themselves. Obviously, the time to do this is throughout the project, not at the end.

Giving people the opportunity to decide for themselves is tough. Once you have designed a solution, you may be so wedded to it that you view any resistance to it as a personal attack. You may grow defensive, defiant, or disparaging. You may try to do everything you can to save face. But remember that if you don't give people the opportunity, they'll take it anyway, and usually with disastrous consequences. When you let them decide, they are much more likely to take ownership. You know you've succeeded when they want you to move on so they can do it themselves.

Summary

At the outset of the project, you spend time understanding the situation. That understanding must be maintained and updated as you progress. It requires you to spend lots of time with people at all levels of the organization and to care about their opinions. If your attitude is one of learning rather than telling or selling, the chance that your solution will succeed is much higher.

Perhaps the most challenging aspect of getting people involved is to make them feel comfortable enough with you to be open and tell you what you need to know to understand the situation fully. If people don't tell you what is really on their minds, you will not have the right information to develop a solution that fits. Your job is to develop a relationship in which you are an equal partner in the problem-solving process. You want the client to help with the diagnosis, so you want to encourage him to reveal to you, and possibly to himself, what is actually going on.

Now you can put these skills to work as you use the tools in this part. Trying them will let you see how they work and can be applied to your everyday problems.

USING THE TOOLS

Following are several ways that you might begin to use the tools described in Part Two:

- If you are working on a project, prepare a scoping diagram for it. If you are not, try the approach with a personal situation you are facing. Think about how well your project plan fits with the scoping diagram. Look for gaps and excesses. Do you really have to do everything? Are you doing everything you should?
- Develop a hypothesis relevant to a problem you are currently addressing. List the questions you need to answer to convince yourself whether to accept or reject it.
- Put together a storyboard and data matrix for the hypothesis you developed. Is the story compelling? How efficient is your data collection? How creative is it? Will you be able to check the validity of what you gather?
- Conduct a risk assessment for a current or upcoming project. What could go wrong? What is the chance that it will? What would you do if it did?

PART THREE

DESIGNING THE SOLUTION

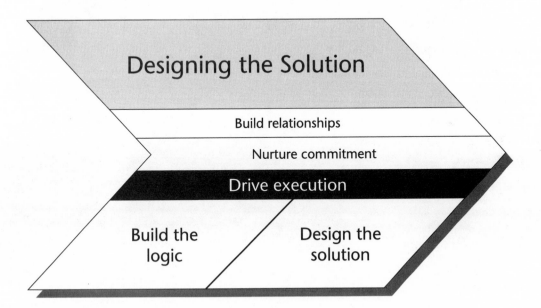

Designing the Solution

Build relationships

Nurture commitment

Drive execution

Build the logic

Design the solution

CHAPTER EIGHT

NOT JUST THE FACTS

Building the Logic

Once you begin collecting data, you also begin developing opinions about the validity of your hypotheses. These opinions start to give you a sense of what you will conclude about the situation you are investigating, which in turn helps lead you to the solutions you might design and recommend. The challenge is keeping everything straight. Which hypotheses do you accept? Which ones do you reject? Which ones require more data? How confident are you of the data you have collected? Which data are useful? Which data are trustworthy? Why are there inconsistencies? Do they matter? You want to move from a morass of inconsistent and unclear data to a set of clear, logically consistent conclusions that lead to innovative and practical solutions. But how?

I learned at McKinsey & Company that a solution is valuable only if it is transparent—that is, if you can explain why you are recommending it—and that conclusions are much more valuable if they are based on facts. The information on which belief or judgment is based makes a big difference. If you show people why you reached your point of view, they have the opportunity to decide whether they agree based on the logic you used. Justification is a big part of action. Making your conclusions and solutions transparent—in other words, showing your work—is key to success.

The premise underlying the designing solutions process is fact-based analysis. Any conclusions you draw and solutions you design are based on the facts that underlie the situation. Unfortunately, facts can be a bit hard to pin down.

While I was working with a durable consumer goods manufacturer once, it took nearly a month before everyone agreed on the definition of a sale. I had thought that a sale was a simple transaction to track. However, it was complicated by returns, manufacturer's discounts, salespeople's negotiated prices (which reduced sales but also their commissions), sales to distributors, sales to end consumers, and so forth. I would never have believed it would take so long to come to agreement on such a seemingly straightforward concept. Then I did a project for a bank. It took even longer to come up with the components of customer profitability. First, we had to define what a customer was . . .

When you move beyond measurable transactions, facts are even harder to agree on. Everyone knows about the unreliability of eyewitnesses at crime scenes. There is no reason to believe that people working in an organization are any more reliable at remembering what they have experienced. And yet we all believe we remember something exactly.

And then there are opinions. Whose is right? Whose matters?

The dictionary is no help. The *Oxford English Dictionary* defines a fact as "truth; reality; a thing known for certain to have occurred or to be true; a datum of experience." For lots of things, it is not at all clear whether it is known for certain to have occurred. It depends on whom you ask. Truth is variable as well. We have all been admonished that perception is reality. Hence, all perceptions are valid. What do you do with varying perceptions when you are trying to conduct a fact-based analysis?

All of these problems with facts notwithstanding, attempting to solve a problem by relying solely on opinion is a much greater risk. Table 8.1 sets out just a few of the mistakes people typically make when they face decisions. My remedy,

TABLE 8.1. FLAWS IN DECISION MAKING.

Poor framing	Allowing a decision to be influenced excessively by the language used for describing the decision
Recency	Giving undue weight to the most recent information
Primacy	Giving undue weight to the first information received
Probability	Overestimating the probability of familiar or dramatic events; underestimating the probability of negative events
Escalation	Unwillingness to abandon courses of action that have been decided on previously
Association	Reusing strategies that were successful in the past, regardless of whether they fit the current situation
Groupthink	Overemphasizing group consensus and cohesiveness instead of bringing out unpopular ideas

Source: Adapted from Tversky, A., and D. Kahneman, D. "Rational Choice and the Framing of Decisions." *Journal of Business,* 1986, *59,* S251-S278.

and the remedy of many reputable problem solvers before me, is to get the data and do the best you can to use them wisely.

Developing a logic diagram like the one shown in Figure 8.1 is a way to stay organized as you collect data and begin to draw conclusions and design solutions. It also ensures transparency because it shows the rationale you used. As its name implies, a logic diagram shows the logic of your argument in a diagrammatic form. When you read from left to right, it answers the question, "So what?" What are the implications of these data? What is their relevance to your conclusions and solutions? When you read from right to left, it answers the question, "Why?" Why did you arrive at this solution, these conclusions, these findings?

The logic diagram provides a mechanism for you to check your logic with your team and your client. In fact, members of the client organization should be key participants in logic development and testing. If they don't believe it, why would they bother to implement it?

FIGURE 8.1. LOGIC DIAGRAM TEMPLATE.

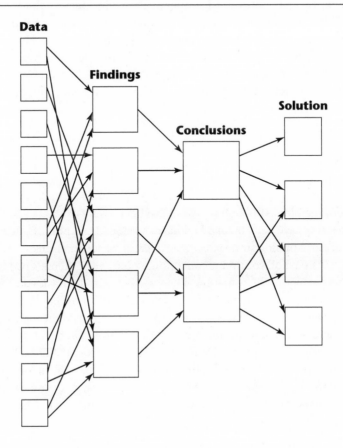

Tommy Lee, a senior vice president at JP Morgan Chase, has been helping people solve their information technology problems and manage their projects for most of his career, most recently as the head of an internal consulting group. Two of his mantras are, "If you can't draw it, you don't understand it," and "If you can't represent it on a single page, it's too complicated." Logic diagrams force him to represent his idea on a single page. They provide a way to put data into a structure and what he refers to as a "commonsense approach to determine when to get more data."

Hans-Ulrich Mayer from Nestlé feels that "not everyone is honest enough to admit that they are illogical," so logic diagrams help them to see the flaws and gaps in their thinking. One project his area was involved with was improving manufacturing productivity in a line of business across Europe. The project was particularly challenging because different countries had different approaches, different sensitivities, and, for the most part, some arrogance about the superiority of their own way of doing things.

The project manager whom Hans-Ulrich appointed was young, relatively inexperienced, and not European. From the start, he had no credibility with his European counterparts. In fact, in most presentations, participants arrived wanting to prove he was wrong and reject his solutions. However, his logic diagrams gave him fact-based authority. Ultimately, the people affected showed a great deal of appreciation for the work, Hans-Ulrich believes, in part, because of the strength of the project manager's methodology and the logic diagrams he developed.

The Details

Let's say you are working with Acme Ceramics, which makes and distributes ceramic tiles. Although its sales have been rising dramatically year over year, its margins have been falling. You have developed a hypothesis that the absence of a sales and pricing strategy is the root cause of low margins.

As part of your data collection, you divided Acme's product line into two groups: high and low margin. Then you organized the sales data into these groups. One piece of very low-level data might show that three boxes of Acme's low-margin tiles were sold at the hardware store at the corner of Main and Maple in Springfield yesterday. The data for the previous month from all the hardware stores the company supplies could be summarized into a statement about sales in that month. A comparison of this to sales the month before, the year before, and the budgeted amount would provide a higher-level understanding of the current situation. Comparing the data for low-margin products to high-margin products is at a higher level yet. Your finding from these data might be that low-margin products are selling at a rate of two-to-one over high-margin products. As the data get summarized, they evolve into findings.

Data

Your logic diagram should contain data to convince yourself, but also data to convince your client, stakeholders, and other interested people. Remember that data do not have to be quantitative to be convincing. Behaviors and opinions are just as important as operating reports and sales numbers in determining the best path for an organization to take. Background and experience will also have an effect on the level of detail required to build the logic for an argument. For example, a client who is contemplating a move into a new product line will need much more evidence about the prognosis for the product than will a client who has been successful in that line for many years. A client who has had a bad experience with the product line may need more evidence than people in either of the other two situations.

You need to be careful to understand which data are news and which are self-evident, not to you as you develop the logic but to those with whom you plan to share it. You may think that some aspects of your argument need no support, but your client, stakeholders, and other interested people may not agree. Conversely, you may think some aspects need a great deal of elaboration, but they are obvious to your client organization. Remember that you have to convince your client as well as yourself about the validity of your logic.

My first consulting project was for an investment bank that wanted help deciding whether a software package the floor traders wanted to buy was worth breaking standards for. Historically, this firm used only software for which it owned the code, and the vendor in this case was not willing to provide this information. One small part of the analysis required us to look at the total cost of using the software over a two-year time horizon. Just as I had learned in Finance class, I carefully calculated the net present value of the initial hardware and software purchase price and subsequent maintenance fees. I provided ample justification for what I perceived to be the superiority of my approach. And although I'm sure my answer was correct, it was way out of line with what the problem and the client required. First, net present value does not add a great deal when conducting an analysis over two years, unless the cost of capital is in excess of 20 percent. Second, telling an investment house about the superiority of a particular valuation technique seems to be bringing coals to Newcastle. Not surprisingly, my manager caught my blunder and gave me my first lecture on working smart and not hard.

Findings

A finding is a summary statement derived from raw data that directs your thinking toward the solution of the problems or the exploitation of the opportunities. When you develop findings, you discard the irrelevant, cross-check the relevant, and use the result to review and revise your hypotheses.

At Acme, you might have conducted six interviews with salespeople who are responsible for ensuring shelf space for Acme's products at mom-and-pop hardware stores. Sales to national chains and contractors occur through a separate channel. Each salesperson had several opinions about the organization, but they all stated that they focus on sales volume rather than margin because of their compensation plan. Each individual you spoke with provides you with a data point. A finding that summarizes the data points would be, "The sales compensation plan favors low-margin products."

Whether the sales force focus is an interesting finding depends on where the argument is going. It begs the question, "So what?" More specifically, what effect does the sales force's focus on low-margin products have on average margin? This finding has the potential to lead to a diagnosis, so it should not be discarded. When a group of findings lead you to diagnose the situation and make a judgment about it, you have developed a conclusion. By themselves, findings do not interpret information or explain implications.

Conclusions

A conclusion is a diagnostic statement, based on the data and findings, that explains problems or opportunities and is significant enough to warrant action. Hypotheses are untested opinions. Hypotheses that are tested and supported become conclusions, but conclusions can also arise directly from the findings.

To continue the Acme example, you have found that low-margin products are selling much better than high-margin products. You have also found that the compensation system favors low-margin products. As you continued data collection, you found that Acme's marketing and advertising do not distinguish between high- and low-margin products. Finally, you have found that Acme is underpricing its competition by a significant amount on its low-margin products and charging a significant premium in relation to the competition on high-margin products. Your initial hypothesis about the absence of a sales and pricing strategy seems to be well supported. However, to support it fully, you will have to investigate whether there is a sales and pricing strategy and if your findings line up with it. If you find a strategy to focus on high-margin products, your conclusion would be that organizational systems do not line up with the strategy. However, if there were no strategy in place, your conclusion would be your initial hypothesis: A lack of a sales strategy is the root cause of low margins.

Once again, the question, "So what?" looms. Whether this is an interesting and important conclusion depends on where the argument is going. One or more conclusions lead you to design a solution describing what your client should do—what actions he should take. In this case, you might recommend that the organization develop a sales strategy that lines up compensation, marketing expenditures, and pricing.

Solution

The solution in a logic diagram describes the actions that you believe the client should take based on the conclusions you have drawn. Good solutions are practical and achievable, and they will lead to specific benefits when they are implemented. They resolve problems or realize opportunities. It is not until you have included a solution in your logic diagram that you can be sure that the logic is airtight and compelling. A conclusion isn't useful unless it points to an action the client should take. Hence, until you have recommended a solution, you don't know whether you have gaps or excesses in your logic.

At a minimum, a solution should cover the assignment scope. If it is implemented, the client should expect to reach his objective. It should completely cover all the aspects of the conclusions, and you should be able to track its components back to the findings. The solution usually addresses the findings via the conclusions by indicating how the findings will change as a result of implementing the solution. In other words, the findings provide the details that the solution must address, as is the case in Acme's logic diagram in Figure 8.2.

However, the requirements for solutions go far beyond fitting into an airtight logic diagram. The solution must be feasible for the client to whom you are recommending it. There is no value to a solution that doesn't fit with the client's constraints and her will and skill to implement. Chapter Nine provides details on how to design solutions in the light of the client situation.

The Logic Diagram

This completes the path from data to solution. Each finding is supported by data, each conclusion is supported by findings, and each solution is supported by conclusions. The logic is airtight.

Reading from left to right in Figure 8.2 verifies that the argument is complete. You will be able to answer the question, "Why?" about the solution using the conclusions that lead to it. For each conclusion, you will be able to explain why you reached it by relying on the findings that lead to it. Finally, although the data are not shown in Figure 8.2, you have data to support each finding.

FIGURE 8.2. LOGIC DIAGRAM FOR THE ACME PROJECT.

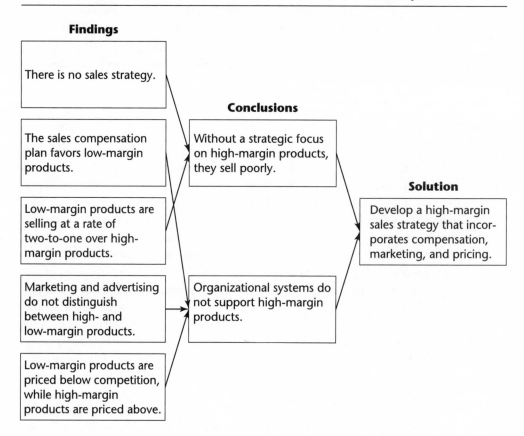

The number of levels you need to move from data to findings depends on the detail required to support your argument. There aren't arbitrary lines between data and findings and findings and conclusions. What is important is that you move from data to synthesis to diagnosis to solutions. If it takes two levels of findings rather than just one, that's fine.

Mike Hastings once worked with a project team that was struggling with sequence and messages in its final presentation. They called him in after working on it for the better part of a week. After thirty minutes, Mike asked them to show him the logic diagram. They had to reverse-engineer it from the messages they were trying to share with the client because they hadn't put one together previously. Forty-five minutes later, they were able to develop a story line and realized they needed only about half of the original slides. They also realized that one area they were pursuing had insufficient data to draw conclusions.

Events, Patterns, and Structure

Another way to label data, findings, and conclusions is events, patterns, and structure.[1] An *event* is something that happens—a piece of information. A sale was made, a customer complained, an employee was late for work. An event takes place at a single instant in time.

Patterns help us to understand how events relate to each other. They are the relationships among events. For example, sales have been growing in the Southwest region and declining in the North, customer complaints have been increasing for the past six months, employee motivation is on the decline. Usually you can create a chart or a graph to describe a pattern. When you think in terms of patterns, you are putting the events in context. You are beginning to answer the question, "So what?"

Causality is the next level of understanding. The generic question is what caused the pattern. What caused sales growth to vary between regions? What caused customer complaints to increase? What caused employee motivation to decline? Answering these questions gives you insight into the underlying *structure* of the situation. Sometimes, however, one level of answers is not enough. You have to probe more deeply to find out the root cause of the situation if it's relevant. In the case of sales growth, if the cause is shifts in population, you may be able to stop investigating, but if it is a change in management or a restructuring of incentives in one region, you may need to dig further.

Of course, if as you dig you find that you don't have all the data you need, you may have to test your hypothesis about the root causes of the patterns of events that you have uncovered.

Building a Logic Diagram

The first decision you need to make when building a logic diagram is whether your solution should be portrayed by a single box or by its elements. Although you are designing an integrated solution for the organization, connections to conclusions and findings may be clearer if you portray its elements.

Assuming you choose to portray elements of the solution, there are only a few rules to follow when creating a logic diagram. If there is a flaw in your logic diagram, there is probably also a flaw in your thinking. There must be arrows from each piece of data to at least one finding. If there isn't a connection (see Figure 8.3), there isn't a "So what?" The same holds true from findings to conclusions and from conclusions to the elements of the solution.

There must be arrows to each solution element from at least one conclusion, to each conclusion from at least one finding, and to each finding from at least one piece of data. If you don't have an arrow, you can't answer the question, "Why?" Although there is nothing wrong with having only one finding lead to a conclusion, it usually indicates a risky diagnosis.

Finally, arrows may not be drawn from findings to the solution elements, from data to conclusions, or from data to solution elements.

The most practical way to begin to develop a logic diagram is to do so as soon as you have created the data matrix. A hypothesis is an unsupported conclusion, and a question that is answered becomes either data or a finding, depending on the level of detail in the answer. Questions to which you hypothesize answers are propositional hypotheses. As you find answers to the questions, you turn questions into data and findings, and as the findings are collected, they provide support for hypotheses, turning them into conclusions (Figure 8.4). The problem with this approach, however, is that you may miss some very interesting data combinations, which could lead to unexpected findings and conclusions, because you have limited your assessment of the data to verifying or rejecting your hypotheses.

Another approach for developing a logic diagram is to collect all the data first and sift through them to develop findings. Then diagnose the situation based on the findings you have developed to create conclusions. In the ideal world, this is the preferable method: rather than let yourself be swayed by your initial hypotheses, you let the data talk to you. However, there is a problem with this approach as well. When you do not construct your logic diagram as you go, you may not recognize that a line of reasoning is flawed. If you don't, you may be

FIGURE 8.3. LOGIC DESIGN FLAWS.

FIGURE 8.3. LOGIC DESIGN FLAWS. (*Continued*)

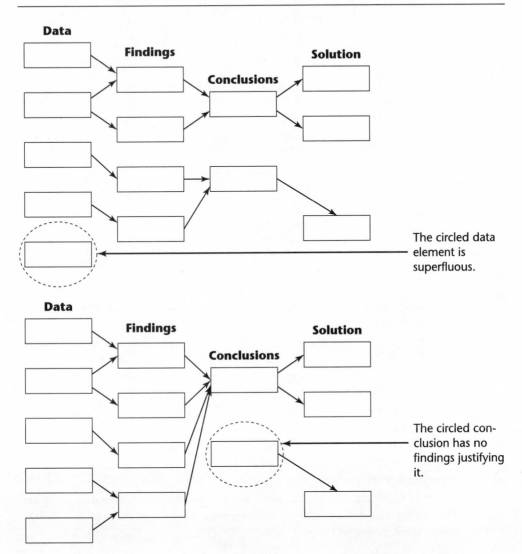

The circled data element is superfluous.

The circled conclusion has no findings justifying it.

faced with new hypotheses and data requirements late in the project. It is possible to overcome this problem by being disciplined about maintaining your storyboard and keeping close track of those stories that are not turning out the way you had expected.

Of course, no matter how you approach logic development, it is important to keep your objective and scoping diagram in mind. It is easy to get sidetracked

FIGURE 8.4. EVOLVING LOGIC DIAGRAM.

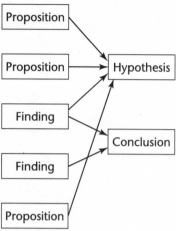

by a potential conclusion and find more data for it, only to realize that it does not relate to the issue at hand. When collecting data and developing the logic for the project, remember that it is just as important to discard data as it is to search for them. Remember also to check your data for accuracy and consistency in addition to relevance. Sample the integrity of your data before you use them. Compare views inside and outside the organization, compare claims made by customers to those made by salespeople, and compare the perceptions of managers and their subordinates.

Logic diagrams, although always useful, are much easier to build when you keep the project's scope firmly in mind. Mike Griffiths once worked with a client team that let their logic diagram grow out of control: they ended up with over five thousand data items grouped under 150 findings. As the team became more and more uncertain about what they were investigating, interviews became increasingly unstructured and inconclusive. Without a scoping diagram to control the project, scope naturally crept outward. The data were so unwieldy that before Mike intervened, the only way the project manager could absorb what had been collected was to spend his entire two-week Christmas vacation studying fifteen flip charts of sticky notes containing the data points. Mike and the client estimated that by developing a scoping diagram and using hypotheses from the outset, they could have reduced the project's duration by more than 60 percent.

Answering the following questions will help you assess the quality of your findings and conclusions:

Do your findings . . .

- Fully test the hypotheses?
- Fully support the conclusions?
- Provide a reliable and accurate summary of the data?
- Seem clear and convincing?

Do your conclusions . . .

- Diagnose problems or opportunities?
- Cover the full scope of the topics?
- Unite the findings?
- Suggest possible solutions?
- Use judgment?

The challenge with these questions, of course, is that they are completely subjective. Something may seem completely clear and convincing to one person and utter nonsense to someone else, depending on their background, experience, and predisposition. This is when your early work on understanding the situation will stand you in good stead. If you have developed a good understanding of the social and political climate in the organization, you will have a good sense of what it is that people are likely to accept and what they are likely to resist. However, nothing works as well as asking people whether they buy an argument, as long as you do it in such a way that indicates that you care about their answer. You have to make yourself confrontable when you test your logic, and you have to listen to what people say. Whenever you are trying to convince someone of something, you have to start from where they're starting from, not from where you'd like them to end up. Appendix B provides insight into how to ask questions so that you obtain insight into people's perspectives rather than platitudes or shallow advocacy.

The Benefits of a Logic Diagram

In addition to the obvious advantages of a logical argument, there are two ways that the logic diagram assists in the problem-solving process. First, it helps you see how far along you are in the data collection process and where there might be holes in your logic. Second, it provides a simple way for you to share your logic with others. Rather than making someone read a half-finished presentation or listen while you talk through your arguments, you can show them your logic diagram and ask them to tell you which parts of it they find convincing and which need more work.

The logic diagram can be shared with people who know little or nothing about your project. You will quickly find out if you are clear and straightforward and if your arguments make sense to others. It's amazing how often you think you have great support for a point of view, only to realize when you share it with someone else that it's not as airtight as you thought it was.

Jeff Gill, the director of human resources for Landmark Graphics, once used a logic diagram when he was the foreman of a jury. After two half-days of testimony, the jury was asked to reach a verdict. Jeff found that they had widely differing opinions about what they had heard. He suggested they make a list of the facts they could agree on and then move forward from there.

In consultant development sessions, my colleagues and I ask participants to go through a case study to learn problem-solving tools and techniques. The sessions culminate with the Logic Challenge: each team is asked to present its logic diagram to the group and stand by silently while the other teams comment. Often what appears completely logical and compelling in a team room quickly falls apart when subjected to the scrutiny of those who are not personally involved.

Summary

The logic diagram is the core of the problem-solving process. By providing a framework to help you connect data, findings, conclusions, and solutions, it allows you to test quickly whether the argument you hope to use to convince your client to act is both complete and consistent. Each component can be tested by itself, but it is testing the whole and answering the questions "Why?" and "So what?" that enable you to determine whether you are really making sense.

CHAPTER NINE

IF YOU CAN'T CHOOSE, YOU LOSE

Designing the Solution

During World War I, German U-boats were a huge threat to the British and Americans. Somebody asked the American folk philosopher Will Rogers what should be done. He thought about it a moment and suggested that the military should boil the ocean.

The questioner was flabbergasted. "Boil the ocean?"

"Yes," said Rogers. "I think if you heated up the Atlantic Ocean, the submarines would rise to the surface and you could capture them." (In another version of this story, he says, "All the water would evaporate, and you could see the submarines on the bottom.")

"But how would you boil the ocean?" the person asked.

Rogers answered, "I'm just the idea man here. I've given you a solution. You go figure out the details."

Rogers's idea is clearly outlandish, but another example shows that sometimes the apparently ridiculous leads to a creative solution.[1]

In the Cascade Mountains, snow is so heavy in the winter that it often causes telephone lines to snap. The problem is exacerbated because the snow also prevents repair crews from driving to the locations of the breaks. In a session to discuss how to reduce the incidence of line repairs, participants came up with what seemed on the face of it to be a nutty idea: attaching heating pads to the bottoms of airplanes and then flying very close to the wires to melt the snow before it got too heavy. This led to the very practical idea that the vibration from helicopter blades would shake the lines, causing the snow to fall off. Implementation saved $8 million per year.

The steps you follow to design an appropriate solution are based on the premise that your first idea is not necessarily your best. Many people have the mistaken notion that they should go with their initial hunches. The reality is that the first idea to solve a problem has nothing more going for it than a first draft of anything else. Taking the time to consider other options will always lead to the best solution. Thinking of alternatives once there appears to be an answer may seem like a waste of time. And all the work that has been done to reach conclusions often makes the first answer seem so blindingly obvious that to push further would be pointless. Gap analysis provides a case in point.

Gap analysis is an approach that has gained a great deal of support in the past decade as a technique to solve problems and improve organizational performance. In gap analysis, as in all other good problem solving, you begin by setting the objective. You then collect data in an effort to understand the current situation. You follow this with the creation of a vision of the future state. Finally, you figure out how to fill the gap.

Gap analysis is logical in theory, but it has several potential pitfalls that make it challenging to execute. First, individuals often get sidetracked. Many organizations seemingly take forever to agree on the current situation, not because individuals lack an understanding of the organization but because their personal understanding is not necessarily consistent with others' understandings. Often the better part of the project is devoted to agreeing on the current state, leaving very little time for moving forward or making improvements.

Second, the planned state is often decided on without the benefit of a logic diagram: an option is put forward, and people assume it is right for them. Most people do not bother to test whether it is an appropriate choice. They move directly to the next step of determining how to get there. If they tested several options first, they would be much more likely to find the one that best fits the organization's objectives and capabilities.

Developing Plausible Alternatives

Nothing is more dangerous than an idea if it is the only one you have.

EMILE CHARTIER A.K.A. ALAIN, FRENCH PHILOSOPHER

The best way to have a good idea is to have lots of ideas.

LINUS PAULING, NOBEL PRIZE WINNER

Centuries of investigation into problem solving have resulted in a clear consensus that the process requires three steps:

1. Understand the problem.
2. Identify alternative solutions.
3. Select the best among them.

John Dewey described them as: recognize it, weigh alternative claims, and form a judgment.[2] And Herbert Simon called them intelligence, design, and choice.[3]

So far, the process of designing solutions has focused solely on understanding the problem or gathering intelligence. Now it's time to develop alternative solutions and select the best among them—that is, design solutions and choose from your designs. Switching from converging on a problem definition and conclusions to diverging to develop alternative solutions not only requires intellectual agility, but is very frustrating as well. Most people want to get on with the job of fixing or improving. Instead, you need to suspend your critical nature and let wild ideas flow without evaluating whether they ultimately will make sense in this context. Remember that if your client asks you whether you considered an idea and you have to say no, the client will always wonder if it would have been a better path to take.

You may be tempted to come up with nothing but straw men once you have developed a solution you like. The way to avoid this temptation is to ask yourself to develop the next best way to reach your objective. You'd be surprised how often the next best way provides insight into a new way of thinking that may become even better than the original solution.

Each of the conclusions in your logic diagram will point to alternatives. For example, you may have concluded that margins can be improved by focusing the sales force on high-margin lines. There are several ways that this can be accomplished, ranging across information, education, and compensation, and all the options associated with each.

To assess which idea or which combination of ideas will work best in your organization at this time requires you to consider exactly what is required to implement each, the likely outcomes you would expect, and the will and skill of the people involved to move forward. In other words, you have to develop each option sufficiently to be able to evaluate it against the criteria that make sense for this particular situation.

Coming Up with Ideas

There are many creativity techniques that you can use to help you get started. Although the most frequently applied is brainstorming, it has some major shortcomings. When people work in groups, social politics takes over. Those who have more ideas, speak more eloquently, or are higher in the organizational hierarchy may intimidate some people. Others become social loafers, thinking that there are enough people in the room to do the thinking work, so they can sit back and let it happen. Still others may have an idea on the tip of their tongues, but they forget it while waiting for someone else to speak.

The major benefit of brainstorming comes from the piggybacking of ideas. Someone puts forward an idea, which gives someone else another idea, and so on. Asking each person in the group to come up with an idea in turn or say "pass" can lessen some of the problems associated with brainstorming, but this is quite rigid for something that has been billed as a creativity session.

Perhaps the biggest challenge with brainstorming is the overwhelming urge to criticize ideas as they arise. It takes a strong facilitator to ensure the separation of generation and evaluation.

I run a session in one of my classes each semester to demonstrate the flaws associated with brainstorming. First, I ask the group to brainstorm a particular subject—perhaps getting more tourists to Cleveland. I give the group about ten minutes to come up with ideas, which I record on the board. Usually, they come up with between twenty and thirty ideas.

Then I split the class into groups of five students each and ask them to brainstorm another topic: getting more traffic to a Web site. In ten minutes, the groups tend to come up with fifteen to twenty-five ideas each. Without overlaps, this results in sixty to seventy ideas in a class of thirty students.

Finally, I ask the class to sit quietly for ten minutes and individually come up with ideas for a third topic: improving relations between information technology developers and businesspeople. Between 150 and 225 unique ideas result. I've run this experiment many times in many different formats. The order of the techniques and the order of the problems to work on make no difference. Having people sit together in a room and individually come up with ideas always maximizes the total number of ideas generated.

Of course, if I had asked students to spend ten minutes at home thinking of ideas, they might have come up with two each if they were a particularly motivated group. The power of the third approach, called the nominal group technique, comes from the pressure of working alone in a group.[4] All of the problems associated with brainstorming disappear, which more than makes up for the lack of piggybacking. And piggybacking can be brought into play when the ideas that have been generated are subsequently discussed with the entire group.

While in class, we never move to the next step of using the ideas to develop real alternatives, but it's not hard to assume that with a starting point of 175 ideas, there is more potential for success than if there are only 20.

Testing Plausibility

After the wild ideas have been generated, you must turn to the task of creating plausible alternatives. It probably makes sense to group ideas into categories and spend time discussing them along several dimensions: useful aspects of the idea, aspects that are missing and would make it more useful, and what has to happen to make the idea work.

You must be careful to design solutions that are not only logical but also possible and practical. Review the situation and constraints that you outlined at the outset of the project. You must consider what the organization is willing and able to accomplish in addition to what it needs to do based on the "why" provided by your conclusions. And you should provide enough detail so that the client finds out how to move forward as well as what needs to happen.

Al Morrison, from A. T. Kearney, is insistent that his teams always spend some time asking themselves if they are right. On typical teams, junior people see the senior directors nodding and become confident that the senior directors' experience is sufficient to test the alternatives. Senior people think, "The junior people have done all this work, they're well trained, and they're excellent analysts. Their alternatives must be fine."

Rather than relying on each other, it is much better to ask yourself, "How wrong do I have to be before this alternative doesn't work?" Ask questions such as, "If the expected returns are only 50 percent of plan, would I move forward?" or "If competitors slash their prices by 25 percent, will the option still work?" In any event, point estimates of outcomes aren't nearly as reliable as ranges, even though they often seem much more accurate. After all, which would you rather have: a watch that is five minutes slow or a watch that is stopped at 2:15? The first watch is never right, and the second is right twice a day.

When disasters happen, it is often because the team has missed a fundamental constraint. Once a team working with a trucking company in California recommended moving from single trailers to triple trailers to reduce costs. The analysis and the logic were impeccable, and all the facts added up. But the police stopped the first triple that went on the road. Triples were illegal in California at the time.

One way to be sure that your thinking is complete is to develop a story around each alternative. If you can describe each choice in terms of a story of how it would be implemented in the organization and what results you might expect, you have a complete alternative. If you can test alternatives, all the better, particularly if a lot is at stake.

A Final Check: Intended and Unintended Consequences

The final check before you evaluate the alternatives is to think about the system in which they will reside. Think beyond what you hope will happen and predict the likely reactions of key stakeholders: employees, customers, suppliers, and competitors. If the organization develops a new product, how will competitors respond? How will you respond to their response? You know how you hope customers will react. How else might they react? What will your reaction be to their reaction?

Think not only of direct cause and effect, as in, "If we do A, B will happen." Think also about the consequences of consequences and how they will feed back and affect your solution. Be sure that your response is not the simple answer, and check again that you are attacking the root cause rather than a symptom. For example, the effect of cutting staff will be reduced costs in the short term, but fewer staff may result in fewer good ideas and a greater need to cut costs next year. Another example of shortsightedness related to costs is the way that many organizations address their product development budgets. If expenditures are based on revenues or profits, the time you feel you do not have enough resources to do so is exactly the time you should invest in product development.

Given all these conditions, you will probably end up with fewer than half a dozen plausible, practical ideas. Be sure you have at least two or three. Then comes the final step in the problem-solving process: choice. You must develop an approach for evaluating the ideas against each other and selecting the one that will best suit this client in this situation.

Choosing a Solution

Kepner-Tregoe, named after the consulting and training company that came up with it, is the method that I first learned to make choices among complex alternatives. It involves developing a list of criteria against which to score the alternatives, coupled with a scoring of the relative importance of the criteria themselves. I once tried to use this approach in a client situation.

Delta (a pseudonym) was the fifth largest insurance company in a southern European country. It employed approximately sixteen hundred employees, forty-six of whom were in the systems department. The company had an NCR mainframe system with 170 terminals attached to it. Annual operating costs were approximately 1.5 million euros. Over thirty-three hundred programs had been written to support the processing of the organization's transactions. Yet the existing systems were completely inadequate. Because the systems department was unable to keep pace with new requirements, new applications were typically partial solutions that did not meet user needs. Part of the development burden was the result of systems that were not integrated and, consequently, were difficult to maintain. It was clear that the entire mess would have to be replaced.

The organization's first option was to bolster the system's department and ask it to develop new systems in-house. However, because Delta was a government-owned company, the salary range was limited, making the recruitment of high-caliber professionals difficult. For the most part, the systems department consisted of long-time employees with out-of-date skills; rare new recruits were usually unskilled and did not stay long with the company. (The average tenure of the systems staff was seventeen years.) Based on the systems department's initial estimates, in-house development would take approximately eight hundred person-months and forty-four months of elapsed time. The systems department expected this alternative to cost about 1.2 million euros.

The second option was to purchase a package that would run on the existing hardware configuration. Unfortunately, only one package, XSA, had been found that would run on NCR equipment, and it would require a great number of modifications to meet the country's complex insurance regulations. There was no local customer support for the XSA, although the vendor, located in Britain, assured us that it would provide adequate support. The XSA screens and reports would also have to be translated. Up to now, four XSA systems had been installed, one on an NCR machine and all of them in Britain. The vendor had not made time and cost overrun information available. The sales consultant estimated that it would take twenty-one months to install XSA. The cost of the package (including installation) was 3 million euros.

Delta's final option was to purchase a state-of-the-art package, INS, that ran on IBM equipment. Although this system had never been installed locally, it had been installed at over thirty sites in seven other countries in Europe. Time and cost overruns had been experienced on approximately 20 percent of INS implementations. The vendors of INS estimated that development would take eighteen months. The cost of the package (including installation and the replacement of the NCR equipment) was 7.2 million euros.

We dutifully developed a long list of criteria to determine which option would best meet Delta's needs. Then we spent many hours haggling with the people in the systems department about the relative weighting of the criteria. Finally, we did the arithmetic and found that the differences among the alternatives were not great enough to choose among them. Although it was perfectly clear to the consulting team that INS was by far the superior product and well worth the associated cost, we couldn't make the numbers work out when we used a democratic process.

The main problem we encountered was the client team's resistance to assessing the risk associated with each alternative and the "right" number to use to estimate the length of time it might take to implement each of the solutions. While it was clear to us that the systems department was incapable of developing a solution on its own, it was not clear to them. And even when we made it clear to the CEO, he was unwilling to jettison his long-time, loyal employees.

It turned out that we were solving the wrong problem. Delta wanted to find a way to help the systems organization work better, not a better way to run the insurance business. No amount of finagling with criteria would get us to the answer the organization was ready to hear. We were choosing among options that it was not willing to entertain. Hence, the first lesson of making choices is to be sure that the choices are real; in other words, be sure the organization is willing to accept them and take action. If the organization is not willing, the choices should not be among the list of alternatives.

Providing valid choices implies that organizations are monolithic, unchangeable entities that are not open to discussion and persuasion. Chapter Ten will discuss how you can tell whether your options are possibilities or not-now, not-ever straw men. The effort that you have undertaken to this point in the process will help you to be sure that, at a minimum, the choices you put forward are based on sound logic.

Assessing Options

If you have determined that you have more than one legitimate option and, consequently, the need to assess various options against each other, there are at least three psychological pitfalls to be wary of:[5]

- Plasticity—when the wording of a question influences the answer provided
- Intransitivity—inconsistency in a sequence of choices
- Design bias—when independent choices influence each other because of the order in which they are made

Plasticity. Most people take larger risks when the potential outcome is negative and smaller ones when it is positive. Which would you choose in each of the following:

Alternative A: A 50 percent chance of gaining $1,100

OR

Alternative B: A sure gain of $500

Alternative C: A 50 percent chance of losing $1,100

OR

Alternative D: A sure loss of $500

Most people choose alternatives B and C even though A and D have higher expected values. The long-run implications for organizations are disastrous. Over time, people will decide organizations into bankruptcy. Whenever there is a great idea, they are cautious; when things are definitely getting worse, they take dumb risks.

At the same time, it is easy to convince people to take the sure loss by couching it in terms of insurance. Most of us would rather have a sure loss of a house insurance premium year after year than risk a huge loss once. You cannot count on rationality when giving people choices. Propensity to take risk and the way the choices are worded have a great deal to do with the answer you receive.

Intransitivity. Most of us would believe that if you prefer option B to option A and option C to option B, you would automatically prefer option C to option A. However, when you are making decisions based on more than one dimension, this principle, called transitivity, doesn't necessarily hold.

Consider the three possible solutions in Table 9.1 and the following decision rule. If the difference in completeness between any two solutions is equal to or less than 10 percentage points, choose the solution that is quickest to implement. If the difference in completeness between two solutions is greater than 10 percentage points, choose the most complete solution.

In following the rule, you would choose B over A, C over B, but A over C, because although A takes three months to implement, its solution is more than 10 percentage points better. In this simplistic example, the implications of making selections based on more than one dimension are challenging.

In reality, the choice is probably still more complex because the trade-offs we make don't run in straight lines. For example, we may decide that 10 percentage points is not enough to warrant a longer implementation, but we may also decide that 20 percentage points is worth it if it takes 50 percent more time, but not if it takes 100 percent more time, and certainly not 200 percent more time, as is the case in the example. There is usually an optimal solution based on several complex relationships that we use expert systems to solve for repeating problems such

TABLE 9.1. SOLUTION DIMENSIONS.

| | *Dimensions* | |
Solution Alternatives	Solution Completeness	Months to Implement
A	100 percent	Three
B	90 percent	Two
C	80 percent	One

as loan approvals, but that most people aren't willing to sort through for a single decision such as which software to select. Instead, they focus on intuition and loud voices.

The committee problem is another example of intransitivity. Let's say that rather than trying to sort through all the trade-offs and arithmetically determine the best solution, you decide to let people rank-order their preferences. The person facilitating the meeting may end up with complete control over the result if there are mixed opinions.

Consider the voting in Table 9.2. Adding up the preferences results in a tie, so that gets you nowhere. You could try to delete options one at a time. If you want to be sure that the solution selected is to speed up development of product C, you must not allow a direct comparison between closing Division A and speeding up development of product C, since three of five people prefer closing Division A. Instead, you would first conduct a comparison between cutting the budget and closing Division A. The option to close Division A would be discarded, and you would be left with three people preferring speeding up development of product C to cutting the budget by 10 percent. If you prefer closing Division A, you'd make the comparison between speeding up development and cutting the budget first. If you really wanted to cut the budget, you'd compare closing Division A and speeding development of product C first.

Obviously, this is a contrived example to make a point. Nevertheless, it demonstrates the hazards associated with making choices.

It's not always clear what to do, but voting is never a smart solution. When you vote, there are winners and losers. It is much better to let the data sort out the differences and if the differences can't be sorted out, to admit that too.

One project team Mike Hastings worked with was in a panic because the main options they were evaluating came out equally. "Mike, how can we make a recommendation to the chief executive?" "You can't, guys. Just tell him what you have found." They did, and the chief executive responded, "Thanks, team. Great job. It is just as I suspected. You have given me all the information I need. I get paid a big salary to make choices like this."

TABLE 9.2. VOTING ON SOLUTIONS.

Solution	VandeRoy	Smith	Ghopal	Chung	Obihara
Cut each budget by 10 percent	1	1	2	3	3
Close Division A	2	3	3	1	1
Speed up development of product C	3	2	1	2	2

Design Bias. Perhaps the most insidious of the problems associated with developing criteria and evaluating options is deciding what to do first. If you develop criteria before you create alternatives, you risk developing only alternatives that fit within the criteria. You subconsciously evaluate at the same time as you create, resulting in stifled creativity and poor choices. But if you develop the evaluation criteria after you have designed the viable options, you may slant the criteria in favor of your personal choice. The best way to separate design and choice is to have different people undertake each task.

Selecting Criteria

The most obvious criteria with which to evaluate options are time, cost, quality, and risk. Although I discussed acceptance earlier in the chapter and no alternative should get this far without being acceptable to the people who matter, I include it again with the other criteria to be sure you've considered it thoroughly:

> *Acceptance*—Are the client and stakeholders willing to take on this option?
>
> *Risk*—How great is the chance that you won't realize the benefits you hope for?
>
> *Time*—How long will the option take to implement?
>
> *Cost*—How much will it cost?
>
> *Quality*—How well does it achieve the objective?

The client situation will provide insight into how to assess these criteria (other than acceptance). Figure 9.1 provides the ends of the continua that you may want to bear in mind. For example, is your client willing to invest in a strategic solution, or is the situation so desperate that a tactical fix is all that is worth considering?

FIGURE 9.1. RANGE OF SOLUTION OPTIONS.

Strategic	←→	Tactical
Leading edge	←→	Tried and tested
Complete or "Big Bang"	←→	Incremental
Painful	←→	Painless
Revolutionary	←→	Evolutionary
The ideal	←→	Affordable
High risk	←→	Low risk

Remember that it will be difficult for the client to implement something over which she has no control. When considering alternative actions, look only at those that are within her realm of authority. If that is too constraining, you need to work with her to involve others in the implementation process.

These items are not mutually exclusive. Most clients would love a painless, low-cost, low-risk solution that provides a revolutionary, leading-edge, and complete answer to all their problems. It would be easier to boil the ocean.

Summary

The key to designing an appropriate solution for your situation is developing alternatives from which to choose. The first idea is rarely the best. Although taking the time to consider alternatives seems to be wasted effort, it reaps significant benefits most of the time. When selecting among alternatives, focus not only on their elegance, but also on the will and the ability of the organization to implement them.

Once a solution has been agreed to, it is important to determine what is involved in its implementation. Giving the client a to-do list with seventeen items on it is unlikely to meet with success. She needs a road map for how to proceed with details about the steps to take and their order, as well as appropriate timing and staffing. Detailing solutions is almost exactly the same as putting together a project work plan. You need to consider what, who, how, and when.

Chapter Ten discusses what you should consider as you plan to implement your chosen solution.

CHAPTER TEN

WHO'S GOING TO DO IT?

Driving Execution

Problem solvers are often criticized for leaving behind solutions that are never implemented. Without question, there are many unheeded reports lying on shelves in companies in every industry and across all continents. Some believe that the reason is that people don't accept the proposed solution, so they ignore it. I don't think that's what usually happens.

The people involved in creating the report and those who accepted it and paid for it usually think it provided good advice. They just didn't act on it. The solution wasn't rejected; it just withered away. Why is a very difficult question to answer. What to do about it is even harder.

Even if you have had an unrelenting emphasis on ensuring involvement and gaining real agreement throughout your project, you do not have a guarantee that the organization will actually do what you suggest. Procrastination may take hold. Although people may find the solution important to the organization, it may not be as urgent as the current crisis, and there's always a current crisis. They may think it's the right thing to do and may even agree to move forward, but they aren't sure how they should get it done. The people who are responsible for the doing may not take the decision seriously or haven't been told why or how they should execute.

Sometimes resistance comes from previous experiences. William Johnson once worked with an organization in the throes of learned helplessness. The company had been working with consultants for years, and nothing ever changed. But nothing ever changed without consultants either. The staff canteen was a case in point.

For years, employees had been complaining about the canteen's huge high-calorie, low-flavor meals. Nothing had ever been done to improve the food's quality or healthfulness. William suggested that the managing director of the company fix the canteen without any fanfare, just to demonstrate that change was possible. The next weekend, a salad bar was installed, and the kitchen was retooled to enable grilling. Employees felt energized by the evidence that change could happen and felt that they could attack more difficult problems with confidence. It also helped when it dawned on several of them that William was behind the canteen changes. They began to trust him as someone who kept their best interests in mind.

Although there are no guarantees, preparing well for implementation will minimize the chance that the solution withers away. Two elements are required: a justification and a plan of action.

A Justification for the Solution

The logic diagram provides a diagram of the justification for your solution. However, it doesn't usually provide enough detail to be a compelling argument that stands on its own. For that, you need a final report.

The final report is an excellent discipline to hold yourself to even if you never present it to anyone. To be complete, it must contain what, why, and how: a description of the solution you have designed, the rationale for its design or selection, and an overview of how it ought to be implemented. Whether the detailed implementation plan is included depends on the style of the organization you are working with.

Consider All Communication Objectives

Lots of consulting firms provide only a PowerPoint presentation as a final report. Although this sort of presentation is fine for a meeting in which the final solution is discussed, it usually doesn't have enough detail to leave behind. Often people will place a caveat on the cover such as, "This presentation is incomplete without the accompanying verbal comments." Six weeks or six days later, people won't remember the verbal comments. If you want to be thorough, you need to annotate the PowerPoint presentation or augment it with a written document.

The problem of fading memories may not be as acute when the problem solver and the client are both members of the same organization. Nevertheless, people still forget. Documenting rationale never hurts.

I once did a project with a petroleum company in Malaysia. No member of the consulting team was going to be very accessible after the end of the project: e-mail was not yet ubiquitous, and team members lived all over the world: in Japan, Germany, the United States, and Canada. In addition to the usual horizontal presentations we prepared at the end of each phase of the assignment, we left behind a 20-page executive summary and a 110-page detailed description of the solution, its justification, and the steps for implementation. I had been resistant to the idea of preparing a report because I thought it would take a long time, make us more vulnerable to criticism, and never be read. I was wrong on all but one count. The report took forever to write. However, it made us absolutely sure that both we and the client understood what we were recommending and the detailed implications of those recommendations. I can't be sure that anyone ever read the whole thing, but I do know from the Christmas cards I received for years afterward that the project was successful.

Although it may not be necessary to write a book every time you finish a project, it is important to provide enough detail to the client so people can reconstruct the why as well as the what and the "So what?"

Start with Your Storyboard

If you have been following the problem-solving process presented in this book throughout the project, you will have developed a storyboard and filled in the details as you collected the data. At the end of the project, you can use these pages to create the final report.

The order and amount of detail you use depends on how well you have been able to bring people along throughout the project. If acceptance and understanding are widespread, there will be less need for great detail. However, if people still need to convince themselves that this is the right way to go, detail will be necessary and expected.

Detail takes many forms. Jeremy Raymond was once hired by a government ministry to improve its cost management system. One of the questions he investigated was how the current system of cost codes was administered. Quantitative analyses showed about a 30 percent error rate on the codes entered into the system. One accounting clerk he had interviewed told him that whenever the cost code was not on the form he was working with and he didn't know it from memory, he looked out his window to find random digits from one of the license plates in the parking lot. When Jeremy presented his findings, the reaction after the error rate slide was a combination of boredom and incredulity: "I've never had a problem with wrong cost codes!" Then he presented his qualitative findings. Ears perked up, and support for the new processes was quickly forthcoming.

Know Your Audience

Competent lawyers never put their own witnesses on the stand without knowing exactly how they will respond to each question they are asked. Similarly, good problem solvers never put together a final report or presentation without knowing exactly how all the key stakeholders will respond. It makes no difference whether they are in the room. If the solution is important to their future, they will find out about it, make a judgment, and act on it. It is much better to know that judgment ahead of time than to be caught off-guard after the fact.

Mike Griffiths once worked with a firm in oil and gas exploration and production that was not seeing tangible benefits from R&D investments. R&D had interesting ideas, but had never gained buy-in for them from the business units prior to moving on to the next project. It turns out that the business units were afraid of anything that was untested in the field. "I don't care if it works on your computer; you're not putting it down my well!" was the typical response. Mike and his team realized that R&D had to change its philosophy from pioneering groundbreaking technology to implementing innovation on demand. When R&D focused on developing very specific solutions to known problems, they achieved performance breakthroughs in a timely and cost-effective manner.

In short, it is important to maintain your focus on the situation and your stakeholder analysis. Make sure that they are kept up-to-date so that you know where you stand when it comes time to prepare communications.

Once you determine what you want to put into your report, you have to decide how to present it. Three things are important: structure, style, and story. Accurate grammar, punctuation, and spelling should be automatic.

Structure Your Report

The basic structure of reports will always be the same. You begin with the objective of the project and then describe your solution or conclusions. Lots of problem solvers start with a detailed description of what they did, which is usually about as interesting as a summer vacation you didn't take. If you feel compelled to demonstrate that you worked hard, put the details in an appendix.

Focus on Audience Needs. To be able to start with your solution, you need an audience that is on board. They have to be familiar with and supportive of your recommendations. If they aren't, the first question they will ask is, "Why?" and they won't hear another thing you say.

Starting with conclusions, rather than the solution, gives you the opportunity to set context first. You can explain what the problem is or what the opportunity is, and follow that with a justification for why that is the problem or opportunity. Only when everyone understands the logic behind your conclusions do you move to the solution proposed. Figure 10.1 shows a sample report structure that begins with conclusions.

An audience that is already supportive may be more interested in how than why. In this case, you move from conclusions to the elements of the solution. There is no point going into laborious detail and supporting data if everyone is ready to move forward. You can leave the findings and supporting data to the appendixes.

Although you may be tempted to start with some incontrovertible facts leading up to findings and then conclusions, the structure of the report is much easier to follow if it begins with the conclusions and works back to the findings and data. If you start with data or findings, people have no context in which to place them, they don't know why they're important, they can't remember them, and they may tune out during their recitation. If you start with conclusions, the audience can decide whether the findings support them and whether to pay attention based on their level of agreement with the conclusions themselves.

Show Your Logic. The structure should be such that you show the logic you used to arrive at each conclusion in turn. There are only two ways to provide support: deductively and inductively. A deductive argument starts with a position and builds on it to reach a conclusion. A summary statement that incorporates the conclusion is used to introduce the argument. Figure 10.2 provides an example. The argument in this example may be enough for an audience that already agrees with the three deductive points. More commonly, however, the audience is interested in support for each finding.

An inductive argument is based on the preponderance of the evidence rather than a logical argument. Inductive arguments present specific details in support of the overall point being made. Figure 10.3 provides an example.

If you believe the client needs more evidence to agree with any of the findings, you can provide it in the same manner, either deductively or inductively.

In the real world, arguments are rarely so complete or one-sided, however. In the interest of enabling open and honest dialogue about the logic supporting the conclusions, it is important to inform the client about contrary evidence as well. In the example in Figure 10.3, a negative finding might have been, "In the past year, we lost several customers because they felt we were not providing the service that we had promised." This finding would necessarily change the conclusion to something like, "When we resolve our service issues, we will be in a position to sell on the basis of service rather than price." However, this second conclusion would require some evidence that the organization will be able to resolve the service issues . . . And so it goes. Nailing down your logic before you confirm the structure of your final report is clearly important.

FIGURE 10.1. SAMPLE REPORT OR PRESENTATION STRUCTURE.

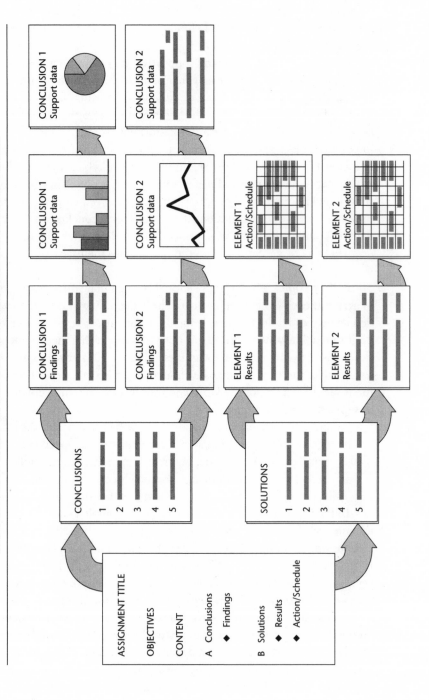

FIGURE 10.2. DEDUCTIVE ARGUMENT.

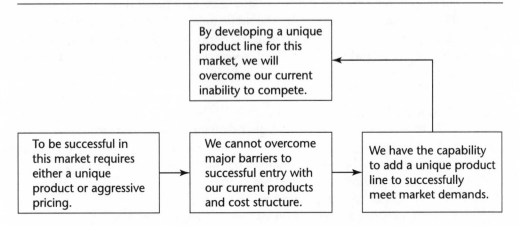

FIGURE 10.3. INDUCTIVE ARGUMENT.

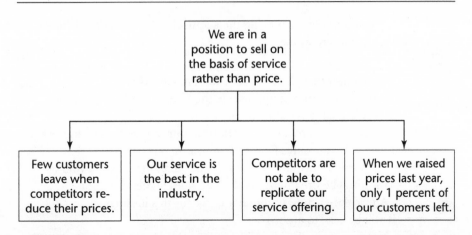

Follow the Rules. Because they are based on human attention limitations and logic considerations, the rules for scoping diagrams and work breakdown structures also work for report structures:

- No level of your report should have more than seven components.
- Consider horizontal and vertical logic.
- Be sure that individual components are mutually exclusive.
- All the components together should be collectively exhaustive.

These rules imply that if you have more than seven supporting points for a conclusion, you either need to select among them or divide them into categories. They also imply that each point should be independent of the others and that all of them are required to provide the entire logic for your conclusion. For example, the following list might be the points you have supporting an acquisition that you are recommending:

- Growing sales in Latin America
- A return on investment that is higher than the industry average
- Similar control processes
- An acquisition that will benefit from our sales expertise and branding
- Little competition outside the United States
- No change in operating managers
- Earnings before interest and taxes/sales higher than ours
- A price-to-earnings ratio that is low for this industry
- No overlapping product lines

The argument for making the acquisition would be made more compelling by dividing it into groups:

- The acquisition will grow faster than the industry
    Little retail competition outside the United States
    Growing sales in Latin America
    An acquisition that will benefit from our sales expertise and branding
- It will have a positive financial impact on our company
    A return on investment that is higher than the industry average
    Earnings before interest and taxes/sales higher than ours
    A price-to-earnings ratio that is low for this industry
- It will be easy to absorb
    No overlapping product lines
    No change in operating managers
    Similar control processes

Groupings can also be displayed graphically. The top diagram in Figure 10.4 illustrates a run-on report with one conclusion and thirteen points to support it. The second diagram shows a grouped structure that you might use if all thirteen points are required. It shows a conclusion (C) with three major supporting points (S1, S2, S3). The first major point has four points supporting it (1, 2, 3, 4), the second has two (S2.1 and S2.2), and so forth. The boxes labeled with an S signify

FIGURE 10.4. RUN-ON AND GROUPED REPORT STRUCTURES.

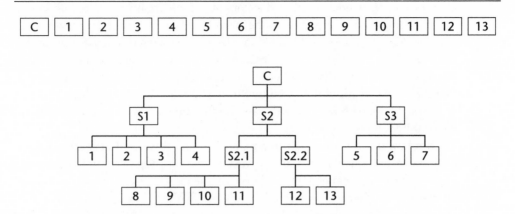

the headings in your communication, and the numbers 1 to 13 signify the details of support.[1]

Use the Appropriate Style

The style that you use for your report depends on what you are trying to accomplish and where the audience is in terms of agreement and commitment. For example, *must* and *should* are much stronger than *might* and *could*. The active voice is more assertive than the passive. Chapter Three provided insight into how to determine the appropriate style for your communication.

Tell a Story

A story makes your final report much more compelling. Stories make information easier to remember and more believable.[2] Both are important if you want to develop people in the organization who are prepared to champion the solution. They need to have the information available to them to give to other people, and they have to be believable. If champions cannot remember the details, those they talk to will be forced to make up their minds even though the logic of the solution may not be available to them.

If all you present are the facts and findings without a compelling picture of what it will be like when the solution is implemented, people will be less likely to be convinced. Research into stories shows repeatedly that a story convinces people more than do the facts alone.

In one experiment, a group of M.B.A. students was asked to evaluate the truthfulness of an advertisement about a California winery emphasizing that the winery used the same techniques as in the Chablis region of France.[3] One-third of the students received a story about the organization in addition to the ad, telling about the owner's father who had "spent most of his life growing grapes in Chablis"; one-third received a table summarizing techniques used at the winery, at other California wineries, and in the Chablis region; and one-third received both. Those who read only the ad and the story were most convinced that the ad was truthful, followed by those who read the ad, the story, and the statistics. Those who read only the ad and the statistics had the lowest faith in the truthfulness of the ad.

But how do you tell a story in a report? Jeremy Raymond's experience with quantitative and qualitative findings provides one way. Rather than just focusing on the numbers, tell anecdotes and provide the audience with quotations from interviews. Another way is through headlines. Rather than labeling charts and sections with descriptions of what they contain, label them with the point you would like to get across. A well-constructed report or presentation should make sense and tell the story even to those who only read the headlines. Headlines also give you an opportunity to direct the audience's attention. Figure 10.5 demonstrates their value. When there is no title (as in Figure 10.5A), the audience is forced to draw its own conclusions—in this case, even about what the graph depicts. When there is a topic title (as in Figure 10.5B), at least the graph is a bit easier to understand, but a headline (as in Figure 10.5C) is clearly the most effective way to direct the audience to the message.[4]

Plan of Action

Once a solution has been designed, the problem-solving process begins again. However, now the focus shifts from what needs to happen and why to how. You still have the same objective, although it may have been refined throughout the process. It may be beneficial to develop a scoping diagram and hypotheses and questions, particularly if you haven't been able to be inclusive in nurturing commitment. For example, you may have developed a wonderful strategy for reducing costs in the call centers, but you haven't visited all of them to uncover idiosyncrasies peculiar to specific locations. Your hypothesis might be that this approach is broadly applicable, but now you have to visit the call centers to test its validity locally.

Another example relates to a decision about how to implement. You may have a choice to implement a particular process improvement or new product one region at a time or across the company simultaneously. You would develop a hypothesis about which approach is better and then develop the questions to decide

FIGURE 10.5. VALUE OF HEADLINES.

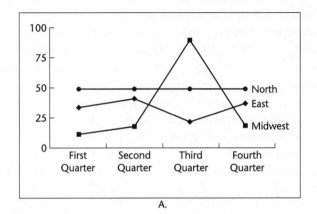

A.

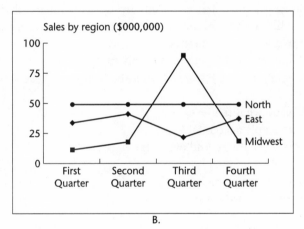

B.

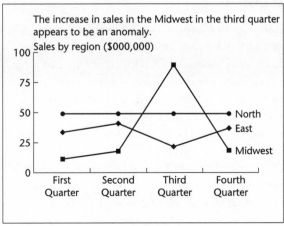

C.

which approach makes the most sense in this context. Will you get more benefit from having a small group of experienced trainers travel from location to location or from having consistency across the entire organization sooner?

At a minimum, you will need to develop a plan. You can begin by following the guidelines in Chapter Six. Pay particular attention to the section on risk in that chapter. Being prepared for setbacks is one of the main elements of a good implementation plan because setbacks are inevitable.

Jeremy Raymond once worked with a high-end sports retailer to reengineer its buying and merchandising. Senior management was very pleased with the outcome of the assignment and asked Jeremy and his team to stay on to help with the implementation effort. They agreed on a price for the work of $350,000. Suddenly the retailer experienced a huge decline in profitability because of a major competitive incursion. The retailer still wanted help, but now had only $75,000 to spend. Jeremy devised a two-day course on how to design a training course for implementers to help the company move forward. Although the fee reduction seemed like an insurmountable setback at first, the final result was much better because it wasn't consultant led.

Although the steps in an implementation plan are dependent on the nature of the solution, six control elements are necessary to the success of every project:

- Measure what matters.
- Hold people accountable.
- Build on enablers, and overcome barriers.
- Establish discipline.
- Plan to make changes.
- Conduct a postproject review.

Measure What Matters

As we discussed in Chapter Two, objectives that are SMART are more likely to result in a successful project. Often, however, progress toward them is too slow to use as the only measure of performance against an implementation plan. You have two options: agree to measure progress on activities that are intended to lead you to the objective or measure intermediate results. When you measure activities, you can determine how much was done: how many people were trained or how many customers were contacted. However, these measures do not provide a complete sense of progress.

There are hundreds of stories about projects from computer systems, to new product developments, to process improvements, in which everything was on time and all intermediate deadlines were met and deliverables delivered, right to the last minute when it was suddenly discovered, much to everyone's dismay, that the project was months behind schedule.

Measuring results rather than activities avoids being deceived by action that isn't leading to the objective. For measurement to be helpful, it has to focus on the performance of the unit or organization: how much time has been saved so far, how much costs have been reduced, how many more products are being purchased. If the implementation is one in which intermediate results are not easy to discern, change the implementation. When objectives and measures are too vague, too distant, or too many, nothing happens. Without concrete intermediate measures, you will never know if you're getting to where you need to go at the speed that you need to travel.

Hold People Accountable

A way to avoid the challenges of implementation is to not be held accountable. If the boss isn't focused on what needs to be done, no one else will be either. Everyone involved must be clear on what is expected by when and how they will be measured. Then someone will have to check up on them to make sure that they have met their commitments. This may seem obvious, but without a mechanism to be sure that it happens, it won't. After all, without people doing things, nothing gets done.

Also, make sure that changes and expectations are reflected in revisions to budgets and operating plans. Otherwise, initial gains may be lost and results may drift downward again without anyone being the wiser.

Build on Enablers, and Overcome Barriers

In every implementation, there are factors that will inhibit smooth implementation and others that will help it along. Spend time thinking through each. One easy way to do this is to conduct a force field analysis.[5]

Write the solution down at the top center of the page. Describe the worst possible scenario at the top left and the ideal outcome at the top right. The center represents the current situation. On the right, describe the positive forces, those enabling implementation, and on the left, the negative forces pulling toward failure, the barriers to implementation (see Figure 10.6). Then identify approaches that would improve the situation: strengthen positive forces and weaken negative ones. The approaches you uncover will form part of your implementation plan.

John Savage used force field analysis to help a major brokerage house improve its performance. The organization needed to grow while holding costs constant. After listing the barriers and enablers to this desired outcome, they realized that

FIGURE 10.6. FORCE FIELD ANALYSIS TEMPLATE.

Solution	
Worst Scenario	Best Scenario
Barriers	Enablers

they needed to put a program in place to recruit high-quality brokers rather than just choose from those who applied.

Establish Discipline

Although good plans don't always result in successful implementation, adherence to them, coupled with the discipline of regular progress reviews, goes a long way toward getting an organization to execute a plan. Be sure that there are monitoring mechanisms in place to keep track and that the results are updated regularly. Make someone responsible for keeping track. Also, create a clear and interesting way to show how the project is doing. A thermometer used to measure progress toward an objective may not be fancy, but it works.

Plan to Make Changes

Regular progress should be much more than a review of measurable progress toward the objective and progress on the steps in the work plan, although these should form part of every review. In addition, you need to discuss how to keep things heading in the right direction.

Talk about what you've learned and what you can do to apply your learning as you move forward. At one organization, the first attempt at a training curriculum for major process changes resulted in failure. People were taught their new jobs, but not the context for the change or how their jobs related to the overall objective for the project. Resistance was rampant. When the training program included a module on the overall project and gave people time to question the why as well as the how, resistance decreased, people retained more of the details of the training, and their performance improved commensurately.

Spend time at every progress review updating the stakeholder analysis and situation assessment. Be sure that the right people are involved and that people have the information they need to make informed choices about how to proceed. Listen carefully to resistance. It's rarely completely unfounded. What do people accept or resist? Do they have any unexpressed motives? Do they resist supplying data? Why? Perhaps most important, when thinking about antidotes, don't forget to follow the rules from Chapter Seven:

- Treat everyone the way you'd like to be treated, but remember everyone is not like you.
- Assume that other people are as clever as you are.
- Start from their point of view, not yours.

Also spend time at every review on barriers and enablers. How can the barriers be overcome? How can the enablers be used to full advantage? Finally, be sure to review new ideas and approaches that you might test.

No matter how much you believe you know how to proceed, there is always feedback. If you are sensitive to it, you are more likely to respond appropriately to the vagaries of your particular implementation.

Conduct a Postproject Review

Except when you are solving your own problem, there comes a time in every project when you must disengage. The project is over, and it is time for the client to get back to business as usual. Often, this is just as stressful as beginning a project, particularly if it has been a long one. In addition to wanting your client to be happy with your work, you want to be sure that the organization is self-sufficient when you leave.

A postproject review signals to everyone that the project is over and you are now moving on. By asking a group consisting of members of the client organization and the project team to reflect on what has happened, you will come to understand how ready people feel to do so.

Prepare questions for the group to consider—for example:

- If you had the project to do over again, what would you change? Could you have predicted some of the blind alleys?
- Is the client happy? What about the project team? Why or why not?

- Did you meet the objective? At what financial and emotional cost? Was it worth it?
- How good was the work plan? Did you stick to it? Would you do anything differently if you had the chance?
- How has implementation progressed? What went well? How could it have been improved?

Asking people to reflect on their experiences will enable them to come to terms with the outcomes of this project and to build their capabilities for future endeavors. By giving yourself time to reflect on the experience with them, you have a much greater chance of doing a better job the next time. All of us can afford to improve. However, the process will be successful only if there is no finger-pointing or "only if-ing." Its purpose is learning, not judgment and recrimination.

Summary

Success begins with a compelling justification and is followed by a clear and detailed plan of action and precise execution. Even with insight, discipline, flexibility, and patience are required to ensure that the solution is implemented and the benefits realized.

USING THE TOOLS

You have now learned about all the tools you need to become skilled in the *Designing Solutions* process. However, it is only with practice that you will obtain mastery. Following are some ideas for exploring the tools described in Part Three:

- Outline the argument supporting a conclusion you have recently reached. Test the argument with your colleagues. Do they believe it? Did you provide enough evidence? Did you provide too much?
- Put together the logic diagram for a recently or nearly completed project. How airtight is the logic? Determine whether it answers "Why?" and "So what?"
- Conduct a force field analysis for a situation you are facing. How can the barriers be overcome? How can you capitalize on the enablers?
- Review a recent presentation. Does it have a clear structure? Is its style consistent with your communication objective? Does it tell a story?

CONCLUSION

That's it! You now have the tools and the process to design solutions efficiently and effectively. In the Introduction, you first encountered the Designing Solutions Tool Kit. I reproduce it here as well. As you will now recognize, it displays the entire problem-solving process. You begin by understanding the situation and the needs of your client. Then you agree on the objectives of the project and determine its scope. Using the scope to manage the project, you develop hypotheses and questions to test your hypotheses. This leads you to a matrix of the data sources you will tap to answer your questions. The matrix, in turn, leads to your project plan. When you have collected the data, you develop a logic diagram that shows how you have synthesized the data into findings and how the findings have enabled you to draw conclusions. Your conclusions lead to your solutions and action plan. Although it's not displayed on the diagram, throughout the entire project your focus on building relationships, nurturing commitment, and driving execution will affect the success of your work. Without relationships, commitment, and execution, no solution is complete, nor can it be implemented.

Diagrams and templates are linear and two-dimensional. Projects never are. Your challenge is to take what you have learned and modify it so that it works for you in each situation you encounter. Every project and every client is different, and each requires a customized approach. If you're disciplined, you'll find yourself looping back: changing the objective as you develop your work plan,

THE DESIGNING SOLUTIONS TOOL KIT.

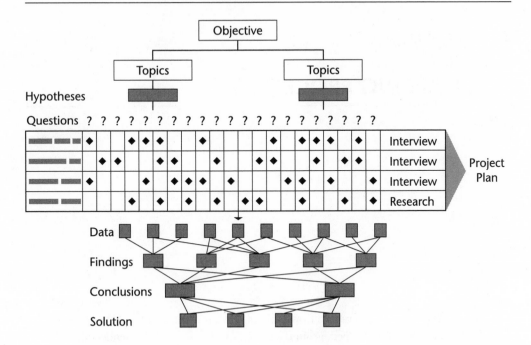

rethinking scope once you've developed hypotheses, developing new hypotheses as you build your logic diagram. That's what's supposed to happen. It's up to you to determine how to use the tools and the process to address the problems and opportunities you face without adhering to them so rigidly that your execution becomes mechanical.

Problem solving is not an art, and it's not a science. It's a craft that requires discipline, enthusiasm, flexibility, patience, and commitment. You've gotten through this book on your reservoir of those. Now it's time to get to work.

APPENDIX A

MAPPING PROCESSES

Aged cheese is removed from storage and tempered to 60°F. After tempering, the cheese is dumped, ground and conveyed to the ribbon blenders to make the various formulas. From the ribbon blenders, the product is discharged to the twin-screw hopper, which force feeds the WCB rectangular flanged timing pump with variable speed control. The timing pump provides the motive force to control the flow through the WCB scraped surface heat exchanger (SSHE) prior to de-aeration. The SSHE uses pressurized hot water as the heating medium to minimize product fouling due to the high protein level in the various cheese formulas. The de-aeration vessel removes entrained air for consistent slices and loaf packaging. From the de-aeration vessel, the product flows to the hot water jacketed scraped surface surge tank to provide continuous flow to the packaging equipment.[1]

This description provides all the reason anyone needs to learn how to map processes. Even if you know what all the equipment is and does, the combination of activities, flows between activities, and the rationale for using particular equipment makes for very difficult reading. By diagramming the process, you clear up the confusion between flows and activities, and even if you don't know the first thing about making processed cheese, you can get a sense of what is going on (Figure A.1).

FIGURE A.1. PROCESSED CHEESE PROCESS FLOW.

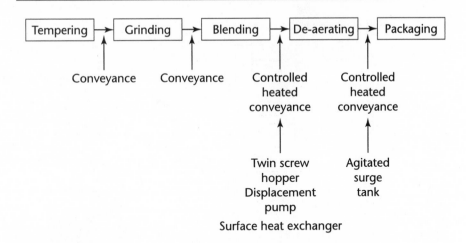

In Chapter One, we discussed transformation processes. Recall that a transformation is always expressed as a process in which some entity (the input) is changed or transformed into a new version of the same entity (the output). Transformations consist of the activities that cause the transformation to happen. Process maps are nothing more than a picture of the activities and the flows between them. In the process in Figure A.1, the input is the aged cheese; the activities are tempering, grinding, heating, de-aerating, and packaging; and the output is processed cheese. Everything else describes equipment or the method of transporting the cheese from one activity to another.

Automated processes are often difficult to understand without a diagram, so people expect to have to diagram them. The trouble with business processes is that often people think they understand them when, in fact, they don't.

There are at least three different representations of every process: what you think it is, what it actually is, and what you would like it to be (see Figure A.2). In addition, each person involved in a process may have a slightly different perception of what's going on. Most people are clear about their part of the process and are happy to discuss it. However, they are likely to give you a sense of the standard process while ignoring or only partially describing exceptions.

Depending on your project, there may be several reasons that you want to diagram a transformation. You may hypothesize that it takes too long or costs too much. You may hypothesize that poor quality is the result of the transformation's complexity or that the transformation uses too much of a scarce organizational resource, such as management attention. Processes you diagram can be as

FIGURE A.2. DIFFERENT VIEWS OF THE SAME PROCESS.

What you think it is

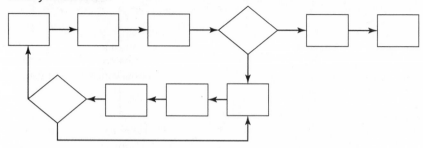

What it actually is

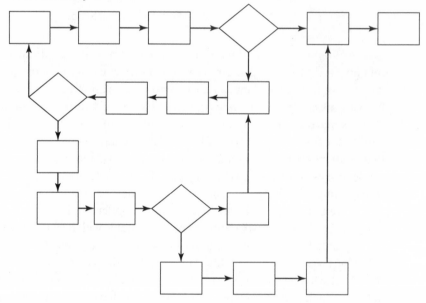

What you would like it to be

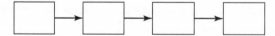

encompassing as the flow of raw materials into finished goods. They can be as specific as the transformation from a customer who has called customer service with a billing question to a customer whose question has been answered. They can be used to diagram an existing process or a proposal for a new way of accomplishing a transformation.

How to Create a Map

Creating a process map is not difficult. Creating one that is accurate is much more challenging. However, by following the five steps outlined in this section and portrayed in Figure A.3, you will clearly define the boundaries of your process map and can begin to fill in the details.

FIGURE A.3. BOUNDARIES OF A PROCESS.

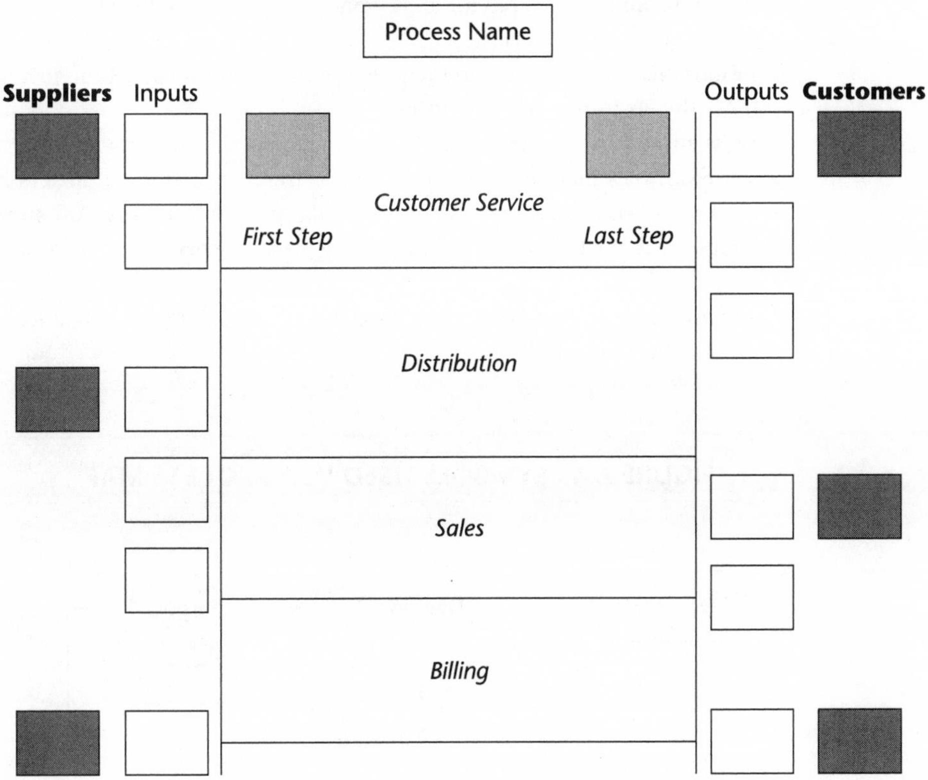

These five steps will help you to create process maps with alacrity and confidence:

1. Identify the transformation you are going to diagram.
2. Create boundaries for the transformation by deciding on the first and last activities or steps in the transformation.
3. List suppliers, resources, and the inputs to the transformation.
4. List customers, by-products, and the outputs of the transformation.
5. List the entities (for example, departments, business units) involved in the transformation.

Only three symbols plus lines are necessary to diagram a process. A box indicates an operation, a diamond indicates a decision, and a circle with an arrow pointing to the line leaving an operation indicates a target, as illustrated in Figure A.4. If you want to indicate the end of a process, you can do so with a small filled-in circle, but it isn't necessary.

Operations are the activities that organizations perform—for example, logging orders, checking credit, paying bills, generating invoices, building products, and answering customer queries.

Decisions always take a yes-no form. Is the order complete? Is the inventory available? Is the customer credit-worthy?

Targets show how the process is evaluated and the expectations for performance. Examples include 100 percent error-free processing, all orders filled within six hours, and one hundred phone calls per week. Figure A.5 shows a process map for a stock replenishment process in a grocery, drug, or hardware store.

There are several ways of approaching the task of diagramming a process, each with benefits and pitfalls.

FIGURE A.4. SYMBOLS USED IN A PROCESS MAP.

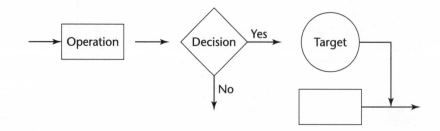

FIGURE A.5. PROCESS MAP FOR STOCK REPLENISHMENT.

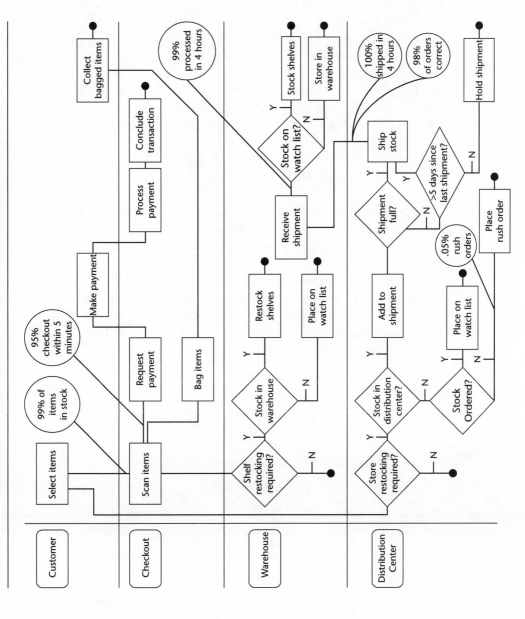

Brainstorm the Activities

Perhaps the fastest way to develop a process map is to bring the people who are familiar with it together to brainstorm the details. You can start by portraying the boundaries on a large wall or whiteboard. Then with sticky notes or cards and tape, you can ask all the participants to put up all the activities they can think of. Ask them not to worry about order or level of detail. When they are finished, group the activities into major blocks or activity areas. Then discuss the level of detail that would be the most appropriate for the task. Organize the activities within each group according to the order in which they take place, discarding any activities that are at too low a level of detail and adding activities if not enough detail has been provided. Figure A.6 shows how you might illustrate different levels of detail. You would probably put each level on a separate sheet.

There are both benefits and pitfalls to using this approach. First, it is fast. Second, because everyone who is involved in the process has helped to diagram it, they will probably take ownership for the end result. However, it is also risky.

If the right people aren't in the room, you might miss a key activity. Even if everyone is there, some key exception processing might get missed. In addition, you may run into groupthink or social loafing. People may agree that the process is accurate just to get along, or they may assume that someone else will expend the mental effort to make sure the depiction is correct.

FIGURE A.6. PROCESS DETAILS.

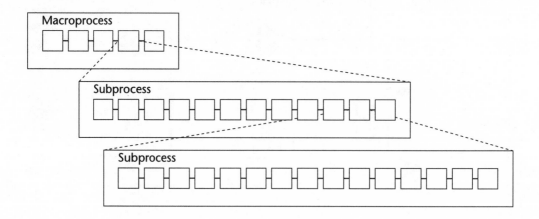

Interview the Participants

Another approach for developing a process map is to interview everyone or at least exemplars of all the people involved in the transformation. If you are an effective interviewer, you will uncover most of the details you want to map by talking with those who are involved. However, there are two problems with this approach.

First, interviewing is time-consuming. If you interview only management, you may not capture what really happens and you may not capture sufficient detail. If you interview a representative cross section, you may be interviewing many people depending on how large the transformation is. In addition, you will have challenges reconciling differing opinions about what really happens.

The second problem is that the result will be your map, not anyone else's, and you may have a hard time garnering agreement and support. No matter how many times you verify your perceptions, there will be people who don't think you've captured the transformation precisely.

Watch the Transformation in Action

Starting long before Frank and Lillian Gilbreth's time and motion studies in the early part of the twentieth century, people have been watching other people perform activities in order to help them improve processes. Watching and asking lots of questions will give you a good sense of what's going on as long as the activities are conducive to observation. Listening in on customer service calls may provide insight into a process, but only if you hear both sides of the conversation and can see the actions that the customer service representative takes. Watching someone write a marketing plan probably won't offer you much understanding.

Create a Tracking System

Creating a tracking system may provide you with the most detailed and comprehensive understanding of a transformation. However, it is also a big commitment. Before you begin, be sure you need the level of detail you will generate.

On one of my assignments, I was charged with reducing the cost to process transactions in a group health claims processing office. We conducted a few interviews but got absolutely nowhere. People shared anecdotes about what they did with the transactions, but no one had any sense of where time was being spent. Then I watched a few people working. Besides hearing lots of complaints about how arbitrary the computer screens were, I didn't get much insight, but I did get very bored. I quickly realized that it would take far too long to see every different kind of claim that the office processed pass through every single step.

We decided to put dots on the claims. Every time someone touched a claim over a two-week period, they put a colored dot on it and on the dot wrote the date and time that they completed their work. After two weeks, we collected all the claims that had been processed and calculated how much time each claim spent in each processing step. What we found out led us directly to the solution. We found that most claims went through the process rapidly—usually in less than a day. Those that required exception processing languished in several locations and were touched by many more people. We calculated that they cost as much as fifteen times more to process. Management was appalled by how many claims fell into the exception category: over the two-week period, nearly 40 percent. We also found out that the challenging claims were not randomly distributed among policies.

We made several recommendations: that claims performance be included in policy pricing, that the computer systems be upgraded so that common exceptions would no longer have to be dealt with on an exception basis, and, perhaps most important, that as soon as a challenging claim was presented, it should be triaged to a special unit. Rather than having several people attempt to deal with it, a team would be trained to handle exceptions exclusively. For them, exceptions would be the norm.

In this case, our data collection paid off, but the price was high. Office performance for the two-week period was 5 percent lower because of the effort expended on tracking. And after the data were collected, it took two people nearly a month to process them.

In most cases, it is best to develop a hybrid approach to meet your project's needs for detail, buy-in, cost, and time.

What to Do with the Map

What you do with a process map depends on the hypotheses you are testing and the solution you are designing. At a minimum, you can use it to help you determine the following:

- How the process is measured and whether that measurement contributes to organizational goals
- How many organizational boundaries the process crosses and how many times the process crosses them
- The amount of actual and elapsed time in each step
- The costs (material and people) expended in each step
- The value added in each step

Process Measurement

By including all the targets by which a process is measured on the map, you determine whether its measurement is consistent with the overall goals of the organization. In their book, *Improving Performance,* Geary Rummler and Alan Brache provide a compelling example of what happens when an organization's process targets do not match its overall goals.[2] They describe a company that manufactured and sold paint through a sales force that ordered product from regional distribution centers. The sales force was measured on order volume, distribution centers were measured on logistics efficiency, and manufacturing was measured on yield (the amount of paint produced per production line).

As a consequence of actions taken by each of the three groups to optimize performance against their measures, shipments were made when trucks were full, not when customers needed paint, and manufacturing simultaneously created excess inventory and shortages because they were making product to fill production lines, not to meet needs.

Assessing the entire set of measures rather than each independently helps to pinpoint flaws and potential flaws in a measurement system.

Organizational Boundaries

A process map clearly shows how many times a process travels across organizational unit boundaries. A great many hand-offs are not necessarily a sign of process distress, but might indicate that the steps in the process are so intertwined that people and organizational units get in each other's way trying to get the job done. Or they might indicate that too much time is spent explaining what is going on. For example, if salespeople have to work with pricing, credit, and the order desk each time they negotiate with a client, the selling cycle may be unnecessarily elongated.

If the process rarely crosses organizational unit boundaries, it may be more efficient, or it may be out of touch, resulting in decisions that may be best for the unit but not for the organization overall.

Time, Cost, and Value

The amount of time spent, the cost, and the value added by each step in a process provide a great deal of insight into potential opportunities and problems. Although there are no rules of thumb about the right numbers and relationships, comparisons and expectations will help to guide hypothesis testing and solution design. In addition, it is always worth considering the amount of time and effort devoted

FIGURE A.7. EVALUATING A PROCESS.

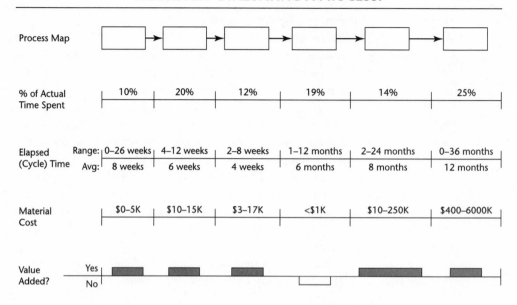

Process Map					
% of Actual Time Spent	10%	20%	12%	19%	14%	25%
Elapsed (Cycle) Time Range:	0–26 weeks	4–12 weeks	2–8 weeks	1–12 months	2–24 months	0–36 months
Avg:	8 weeks	6 weeks	4 weeks	6 months	8 months	12 months
Material Cost	$0–5K	$10–15K	$3–17K	<$1K	$10–250K	$400–6000K
Value Added?	Yes / No					

to planning, checking, and controlling compared to the amount devoted to execution. While the former doesn't usually result in a large outlay of resources, it may expend a great deal of time and attention for very little value. Figure A.7 shows how you might compare steps in a process to each other.

Summary

Conceptually, process maps are easy to create. The challenge lies in creating a map that accurately reflects what is going on (or should be going on). Once you've created a map, its value emerges based on how well you assess what it tells you about the processes it represents.

APPENDIX B

INTERVIEWING TO COLLECT DATA

Why do we interview? We interview to learn about an organization. We interview to gather opinions. We interview to understand how someone feels about an issue, or what he or she believes about the organization or a particular situation. We interview to ferret out political and social issues. We also interview to verify our observations and test our hypotheses. We interview to get help as we develop options and solutions and we interview to garner support and enthusiasm.

Interviewing is perhaps the most productive of all data collection techniques and is a large part of the effort of most projects. It is also time-consuming and expensive. It takes time to prepare, time to travel, time to conduct, and time to record. And often it takes two people's time.

When you interview, you should be absolutely sure that there is no other way to achieve the results you are seeking. If you are interested in understanding opinions and feelings, you have to determine whether people will share them openly and honestly in an interview format, or if observation of behavior is more appropriate. If you are interested in performance data, an interview may be useful for finding out how to obtain them, but probably not for collecting specific results. Data about customers, competitors, processes, and so forth may also be available without interviews.

On the surface, the interview process is straightforward and obvious. You plan the interview, make arrangements, prepare, conduct the interview, record the interview, and follow up if necessary. However, each of these presents several choices and is fraught with challenges.

Planning for the Interview

To plan for an interview, you answer five questions:

- Why do you want to conduct an interview?
- Who will be best able to help you accomplish this?
- How will you structure it?
- When and where will you conduct the interview?
- What background information do you need to be most effective?

Why Should You Conduct an Interview?

When planning an interview, the first task is to determine its purpose or objective. In other words, what do you want to accomplish? Are you searching for knowledge? Are you advocating a point of view? Are you prepared to reject or modify hypotheses? Are you testing your assumptions? Are you willing to modify or discard them? Are you testing the interviewee's assumptions? Do you want the interviewee to change his or her hypotheses and assumptions? Do you want to make the interviewee feel good? You may have several objectives for a single interview. Making them explicit will give you a better chance of achieving them. Table B.1 provides a summary of common interview objectives that you can use to help you determine what you would like to accomplish.

Although all of these are potential objectives for an interview, informing and advocating are not appropriate as its sole purpose. The best interviews are those in which both the interviewer and the interviewee are contributors to the exchange. If you use an interview solely to tell or sell without garnering feedback, you lose an opportunity to develop both a better understanding of the situation and a better relationship with a member of the client organization.

Whom Should You Interview?

On the surface, deciding which people to interview is a trivial decision: the person or people best able to help you achieve your purpose. If you want to find out about a functional area of the organization, you interview people who are familiar with that area. If you want to find out how well a particular manager is doing his job, you interview people who interact with him. There are, however, challenges associated with making these determinations.

TABLE B.1. INTERVIEW OBJECTIVES.

Purpose	Sample Areas of Inquiry
Collect	Data Opinions Perceptions Feelings
Test	Assumptions Hypotheses Understanding of situation Data quality Tentative recommendations
Explore	Options Possible approaches Tentative recommendations
Generate	Ideas Options
Inform	Project process Findings from research
Advocate	Conclusions Solutions

Because of the time and expense associated with interviewing, it isn't always practical to interview everyone who might have a perspective. On the other hand, you may want to interview people to capture their opinions and to make them feel included, even if they are unlikely to provide any new information. It doesn't make sense to interview someone if you don't care about his or her point of view, but it may make sense to interview people even if you already believe you know what they will tell you. You might want to make them part of the process, and you might also be wrong in your understanding. As a rule of thumb, if there are more than a few people who have the potential to help you reach your objectives, continue interviewing until you no longer feel you are learning, as long as you are sure that those you interview are maximally different in their potential to provide good information.

For example, if you want to investigate customer satisfaction, you need to divide customers into types—by size, geography, product mix, profitability, and sales volumes perhaps—and then interview those representing each type. Statistical significance in interviews is difficult to achieve, but a good sense of whether any new information is emerging will help you decide how many interviews are required. If you find after ten interviews that all the customers are saying nearly the same thing, it is probably not necessary to interview another ten. If, however, you find after twenty interviews that the answers you receive to your questions vary widely, you may need to interview another twenty to determine whether there are outliers in your first group or just a wide variety of opinions among customers.

If you are interviewing people in a department, it makes political sense to interview either a small sample or everyone, but not to interview 80 or 90 percent. Those left out may feel marginalized.

How Will You Structure the Interview?

There are many ways to approach the interview itself. The choices revolve around medium and number of people involved in the exchange. Each has advantages and disadvantages that you must consider as you think through the best option to achieve your purpose and stay within the project's time and cost constraints.

The Medium. In-person interviews are the best choice for building relationships and getting a complete understanding of the person you are interviewing. Telephone interviews lack richness because you can't see each other. It is difficult to be sure that the interviewee is engaged. He or she might be doing any number of other things while talking to you. Telephone interviews also tend to be shorter because, without rapport, it is hard to keep a conversation going. If you are interviewing someone you have never met before, it is highly unlikely that you will be able to test, explore, or advocate effectively. On the positive side, telephone interviews are economical and are completely appropriate when nuance is not critical. They work well for very focused interviews with specific and concrete questions to be answered. Finally, they work much better if you have previously met the interviewee.

If the technology does not get in the way, video interviews can be an effective middle ground between in-person and telephone interviews. They are richer than the telephone and can be less costly than in-person interviews, depending on geography.

People in the Exchange. The ratio of interviewees to interviewers revolves around trade-offs between efficiency and effectiveness. As with the medium you choose, the best approach depends on what you are trying to accomplish (Table B.2).

When and Where Will You Conduct the Interview?

Determining the time and location of the interview is usually straightforward, with few choices. The time should be mutually agreed on and should allow both you and the interviewee ample time to get to the location. It should also allow you time afterward to collect your thoughts and review and clarify the notes you made during

TABLE B.2. INTERVIEW TRADE-OFFS.

Number of Interviewers	Number of Interviewees	Advantages	Disadvantages
One	One	Best for building relationships Generally results in valuable information and insights	Difficult to both make notes and develop relationship
Two	One	Best for making notes Provides a check to ensure all topics are covered adequately	Expensive Might intimidate interviewee
One or two (may be a focus group, but not necessarily)	Many	Best for generating ideas and getting responses to potential recommendations Very economical—many people involved at very low cost	Group dynamic may affect data (status, politics, conflict) Comparability of data depends on controlled composition of groups
One	Two	Economic May result in interesting conflicts or disagreements	Difficult to take notes Hard to establish equal rapport

the interview. In other words, interviews should never be scheduled back-to-back, even if they are at the same location.

The interview can be conducted where either the interviewer or interviewee is located, or it can be held at a neutral location. Two criteria are key for selecting a location: the potential for distraction and interruption and the comfort level of the interviewee.

If you choose your own location to hold the interview, you have much more control over interruptions and distractions. You can also provide a more confidential atmosphere. Your location gives greater consistency to the data collection process if you are conducting several interviews with the same type of people. It also provides the interviewee with information about what you do and the way you work.

The interviewee's location provides you with significant information about the interviewee. How she organizes her office, the sorts of items she displays, the books she has, whether her computer is on, what is on her desk, and the kinds of things that are easily accessible give you insight into how she operates. She also has ready access to data and information that might be useful during the course of the discussion.

Because it is the interviewee's home territory, she may feel more comfortable. However, because it is her home territory, you have less control over interruptions.

A neutral location may be most convenient, but it may also be the most distracting, particularly if it is a public place like an airport lounge or a local coffee shop. On difficult or politically charged projects, it may also smack of furtiveness.

What Background Information Do You Need?

Before conducting an interview, it is important to understand as much as possible about the interviewees and their organization. What is their role? Their interest in the project? Their likely attitude? What interviewees say must be weighed along with who they are. Collecting accurate background information demonstrates the interest and respect you have for interviewees. How you collect this information depends on how important it is to have it. For an interview with a highly placed individual, it may be worthwhile to collect information from *Who's Who*, the press, the Internet, and others who know the individual. It is important to know what is common knowledge about the person you are interviewing, as well as where he fits in the organization he represents, what the organization is about, and what others think of him. As an extreme example, journalists can spend weeks preparing for an interview with a celebrity or dignitary.

Making Arrangements

Making arrangements provides you with an opportunity to begin to build rapport, if not trust. By delegating the coordination of interviews, you miss that opportunity. If you can, speak to your interviewee in person to set up the interview. Briefly explain what you are doing and what the project is about, why you would like to interview him, and how you think his knowledge and experience will help. You may have to reassure him about your credentials, the importance of the project, and, particularly for more junior people in an organization, that there are no wrong answers. Then agree on a date, time, and location. Interviews usually last from thirty to ninety minutes. Less time than that does not provide enough time to delve into issues; if an interview goes on for more than ninety minutes, it will be tough to keep someone's attention.

You should be prepared to offer the interviewee a broad summary of the topics you plan to cover if he asks for it. If you have any specific data requirements such as operational results or a particular document, tell your interviewee ahead of time. This will save your face-to-face time for discussion.

Most people are amenable to being interviewed, but if you find resistance, there are several steps you can take. If the resistance is related to a lack of time, make every effort to be flexible. Sometimes, however, time is simply an excuse. If the potential interviewee resists because of a fear of reprisal, reassure him by stating clearly what level of confidentiality you are able to provide. If the resistance appears to come from a lack of interest, you can articulate the benefits of the interview or the project to the interviewee specifically. When you are interviewing customers, it sometimes helps to offer them a summary of all the customer interviews if that is something the client is willing to pay for. Sometimes an introduction from the client is all you need. Of course, if someone really does not want to be interviewed, there is very little you can do but accept his decision and move on to the next potential participant.

Preparing for the Interview

A well-developed scoping diagram, hypotheses and questions, and a comprehensive data matrix provide the foundation for interview preparation. Actual preparation consists of three steps: defining the products of the interview, designing the interview guide, and developing specific questions to ask.

Products are statements describing the output of the interview—for example, descriptions of tasks, processes, and systems; strengths and weaknesses of functions, processes, or departments; measurement approaches and metrics; current and future strategies; customer and supplier perceptions; and interviewee assumptions. Products can be communicated to interviewees in advance without prejudicing their responses. Products do not dictate the type of questions to be asked, but make it clear when you have delved deeply enough and have sufficient information.

The interview guide provides the sequence of the interview: how you will open the discussion, some specific questions you might ask, how you will make the transition from one topic to the next, and how you will conclude. Figure B.1 shows a sample interview guide.

Opening the Discussion

The opening of the interview sets the stage. Its purpose is to let the interviewee know that you understand his business and are genuinely interested in what he has to offer. Remember that the interviewee has to trust you enough to give you the

FIGURE B.1. SAMPLE INTERVIEW GUIDE.

<u>INTERVIEW GUIDE</u>

Interviewee Name and Title:

> Paul Bernard
> Vice President, New Product Development
> IJC Corporation

Contact Details: Room 613, Building C
                          IJC Headquarters
                          22 Navigation Parkway
                          Small City, OH
                          Office: 440.221.3888
                          Cell: 440.819.1313
                          pmb@ijc.com

Purpose: Develop understanding of new product develop-
                          ment role and position in organization

Date: October 19, 200X, 2:00–3:30 P.M.
Location: Dr. Bernard's office

Open
  • Project objectives
  • Interviewee background

Body
  • Tasks and responsibilities
      ○ New product development
      ○ Department management
  • Description of new product development process
  • Strengths and weakness of department
      ○ Systems and processes
      ○ Structure
      ○ People
      ○ Relationships with other departments
          ▪ Marketing and sales
          ▪ Manufacturing
          ▪ Engineering

Close
  • Next steps
  • Anything else?

information you need. In every case, you will want to do the following:

- Describe the objective of the interview and products you hope to collect.
- Reconfirm the time frame.
- Explain why the interviewee was chosen and how he will personally benefit.
- Establish credibility and build rapport in order to put the interviewee at ease and encourage full and candid responses.
- Ask if you can take notes.

Exactly how you cover these five items depends on the situation. You can usually take your cue from what you gleaned when you were making arrangements and the background you have collected about the interviewee.

If you have a reticent interviewee, you may also want to discuss what is going to happen to the information that he will share with you. Remember that all you have to offer is your intellect and your word. Do not promise confidentiality if you cannot maintain it. If your interviewee is the only person who does a particular job in the organization, it will be impossible to keep the results confidential unless you don't use them. If, in contrast, you are interviewing a cross-section of telemarketers, you can probably guarantee that nothing any interviewee says will be attributable directly to him.

During the opening, you must also qualify the interviewee as a source if you haven't collected background information or if someone else made the arrangements. Occasionally, you may find that you are talking to the wrong person for the products you had hoped to collect. If this is the case, the opening is the best time to find out. You can choose to end the interview early, if that is politically appropriate, or you can ignore your guide and conduct a discussion to uncover what the interviewee does know and how he can help you.

The Questions

You have several options for the pattern you will follow in your interview. Generally, you will want to follow a structure that begins with the most general and least sensitive questions and leaves the controversial and personal for last. There are some general structures you can follow within this framework:

Topics:
Standard subject matter divisions based on your interview products.
Sequence:
The order in which events occur (chronology, geography, size).

Causality: Factors and their effects.
This approach is most useful during early stages of a project, when you are
learning how and why things happen the way they do.
Problem and solution:
Identify the objective, goals, and criteria; generate alternatives; and then discuss
how the best might be selected.

For most inexperienced interviewees, it makes sense to develop specific questions in addition to ordering the products. There are only two types of questions
to ask: open and closed. Open questions are broad and unstructured—for
example, "Tell me about . . ." or "What do you think about . . . ?"

Open questions are used to establish rapport or get to potentially threatening
topics in a gentle way. They make it clear that the interviewer is interested in listening to what the interviewee has to say. They allow the interviewee to show his
feelings and talk about his beliefs. Although they give space and freedom to the
interviewee, they may make him uncertain about whether he is answering
appropriately. You cannot predict what you will find out when you ask an open
question and you also cannot predict how much detail the interviewee will provide.
Open questions are particularly effective when you know little about the subject
you are exploring.

Closed questions are designed to elicit a specific reply about a specific topic.
How, when, where, why, is, or *do* begin most closed questions. Closed questions
restrict the range of possible responses. They give more control to the interviewer
but may frustrate the interviewee. They are very precise, but in their precision
lies their risk. You may not ask the right question or not ask a question in the
right way to find out what's relevant. Closed questions make it easier for the interviewee to be glib or even false. Although they make it clear that the interviewer
is thorough at checking what the interviewee is saying, they may be threatening
to some.

Question Types to Avoid. Open and closed questions are not bad or good in their
own right, but there are several forms of them that you should never use. For some
interviewees, a question such as, "Why did you . . ." takes them right back to
what it felt like when they got in trouble as children. "Why didn't you . . ." is even
worse. It immediately puts the interviewee on the defensive. Here are other question types to avoid:

Leading questions.
Leading questions direct the respondent to say what you want to hear rather
than providing you with his own opinion. You may believe that with a leading

question, you are gaining acceptance to your point of view, but any advocacy you achieve will be shallow. High-risk questions include:

"Don't you think . . ."

"Wouldn't it be better if . . ."

"How significant is . . ."

"How difficult was it . . ."

"You can do this by Tuesday, can't you?"

Another form of leading question is more subtle. By embedding assumptions into your question, as in, "When did you start paying attention to scrap rates?" you telegraph your opinions to the interviewee, making it more work for him. Instead of being able to just answer the question, he has to disabuse you of your mistaken assumption first. Often, an interviewee doesn't bother to go through the effort or feels uncomfortable doing so. Even worse, an incorrect assumption can lead to the opinion that you don't know what you're talking about.

You can also lead the interviewee by using biased language—for example, "What do you think about the fruitless focus on Management by Objectives?" The bias tells the interviewee exactly what you think the right answer is, and usually that's exactly what you'll get, whether or not the interviewee agrees.

When conducting an interview, you are attempting to find out about the interviewee and his opinions, as well as collect the data he knows. It does you no good at all to have the interviewee simply tell you what you want to hear.

Multiple questions.

A string of questions or statements and questions results in nothing of value. The interviewee has the option of responding to whichever one he feels like or not responding at all. Your challenge is to ask a clear and direct question and then be quiet and wait for the answer.

Consider this example: *"Can you give me a brief overview of how the department works? Tell me about processes, from whom you get information, to whom you supply information, the end products of your activities, who the key players are, to whom you report, the strengths and weaknesses you face, and what your strategy is for getting through the current challenges."*

Breaking this stream into several single questions will enable the interviewee to respond fully to each one.

Vague questions.

A vague and broad question allows the interviewee to talk about whatever he'd like and doesn't bring you closer to your objective. If an open question is too vague, you have a shotgun.

If you say, "Tell me about yourself," the interviewee has no idea about the context of this question. Should he talk about his job, his family, where he grew up, when he was born, where he went to college, what his hobbies are . . . ?

Too fancy.

You can't help who you are, and neither can your interviewee. Don't put on airs, and don't talk down to him. Use your own acronym-free conversational language. Be careful about picking up and imitating his speech patterns and colloquialisms. They usually sound forced and patronizing. At the same time, be sensitive to the local culture and sensibilities. What may seem to be a perfectly normal question in one context can be cause for a huge uproar in another.

The Best Question Types. The best questions are those that allow the interviewee to express his opinion in whatever way feels appropriate to him. If you give the interviewee the freedom to tell you openly about his opinions, beliefs, and perceptions, you will obtain the most valid data. Several different questioning techniques help to ensure that you have the potential for a rich exchange of information.[1]

Informed questions.

When you ask an interviewee her opinion about specific events and data, you let her know that you have prepared for the interview and that you care about her answers. However, informed questions require you to do some homework beforehand. Here are some examples:

"Sales are down 40 percent from last year. What are your thoughts on what should be done?"

"What do you think about the recent initiative to reduce overhead expenses?"

"How do you think your customers will react to the new product that your competitor has just introduced?"

"This is what we have observed. What is your interpretation?"

Hypothetical questions.

When you want to test a hypothesis rather than telegraph the answer you want to hear, couch the question as a hypothetical situation and ask for a reaction—for example:

"What would you do if you were no longer able to sell through the retail channel?"

"What if the retail channel were your only option?"

"How would you respond to a requirement to cut processing time in half?"

This works best if you give the interviewee an opportunity to react to several choices or to opposites. Otherwise, she might feel that you are simply telegraphing what you hope the final situation will be.

Questions grounded in data.

Ask for specifics or examples of behaviors to make sure that the interviewee understands exactly what you are getting at and that you are sure she understands— for example:

"How many times did *x* happen last week?"

"Can you give me a few examples of customer reactions to the new product line?"

Questions that let people challenge you.

Sometimes you don't know enough about a situation to ask detailed questions that are grounded in data. Don't pretend you know something you aren't sure about. Rather, admit your lack of knowledge, and ask for help in fleshing it out. This is also how you can check the data you have received in earlier interviews or from other sources. Here are some examples:

"Am I correct in understanding that the time it takes to process a transaction varies based on the way that the client fills out the form?"

"I'm not clear about the details of the product development process. Am I right that all ideas for new products go through the steering committee before they are investigated for viability?"

"Are these data valid?"

"What do you think of this explanation? Is there an alternative one?"

Closing the Interview

The conclusion should leave the appropriate tone. You will want to:

- Review what was accomplished.
- Agree on next steps, if any.
- Acknowledge the interviewee's contributions, and thank him for his time
- Ask for permission to call back to check facts or ask for more detail.
- Find out if there is anything else he wants to discuss.

The close is also the opportunity to manage expectations. You don't want the interviewee to feel that his ideas will form the core of your recommendations if they won't. You also don't want the interviewee to feel that you are just ticking him off a to-do list. You should reiterate how his input will be considered as you move forward and give him a sense of when he might hear something about the progress of the project.

You also want to be clear about next steps that are your responsibility and those that are his. Be sure to come to an agreement about when he will provide you with any further information and what form it will take.

Interviewees are good sources for further interviewees. If you are interested in delving more deeply or broadly, ask the interviewee if there is anyone he could suggest to whom you might speak. You might ask him to make the introduction.

Always be sure to ask for permission to call back to check facts or clarify points that you may realize you missed or didn't fully understand as you review your notes.

Once the interview is over and your notebook is closed, your interviewee will be much more relaxed and may open up to you in a way that he never would have during the formal interview. Give him a chance. Always ask if there is anything else on his mind, or if there is a question that you forgot to ask or if he has any suggestions for you. Most of the time, his answer won't be helpful, but it's worth asking for those few times when it is.

Practicing the Interview

The last part of preparation is testing. If you are not an experienced interviewer, it may be helpful to practice with a colleague. If that isn't practical, run the interview in your mind, anticipating the kinds of responses you will get and whether they will enable you to collect your interview products. Check your open and your close. Make sure that your sequence enables natural transitions. Even experienced interviewers benefit from thinking in advance about how they will conduct their interviews. Well-thought-out questions open a free exchange that leads to the information you are seeking, or at least the information the interviewee has to offer.

Conducting the Interview

Good interviews feel like conversations, not inquisitions. You have three tools you can use to make the interviewee feel appreciated and comfortable while ensuring you collect all the data you need: the way you question, the way you listen, and the way you record the data.

The Way You Question. Although I have discussed questions to include and avoid in your interview guide, many of your questions cannot be scripted in advance. You will have to take your cues from what the interviewee says to determine what to say next.

When you are talking with a friend, the conversation flows from subject to subject effortlessly. While it's not unheard of, it is rare to say, "Let's talk about this now." In an interview, it should be just as rare. Instead, you use transitions to move from one topic to another.

The best transitions are natural and feel like conversation. The previous response is the direct link to the next question. Success using this approach requires skill and attention during the interview. The second best way to make a transition is to link the current question to the one that came before. You can develop these transitions as part of your interview preparation. With a combination of inattention and a lack of preparation, the link usually degrades to "Next . . . , " "Another . . . , " "Also . . . , " or "Now . . ."

To ensure that you get the information you need from an interview, you may have to push the interviewee beyond his initial answer to a question. He may have used language you didn't understand, he might not have provided you with enough specific information to be helpful, you may not understand what he is trying to get at, or you may think he is not being accurate or realistic. If you feel uncomfortable for any of these reasons, the best time to check your understanding is right away. That is the way you'd do it in a normal conversation, so that is also the way you should do it in an interview. There are four primary reasons to probe an interviewee:

- *To clarify.*
  If you didn't understand or the interviewee didn't answer the question, ask a clarifying question, for example, "I don't understand" or "What does AFE stand for?"
- *To elaborate.*
  If you thought the answer to the question was naive or insufficiently detailed to be helpful, persist: "Tell me more," "Can you give me an example?" "Any other reasons?" "Hmmm . . . ," or "Uh huh?"
- *To interpret.*
  If you want the interviewee to justify his answer, try, "How do you mean that?" or "Could you explain why that is the case?"
- *To challenge.*
  If you want to engage in a debate with the interviewee about his point of view, ask, "How can that be true?" or "I don't understand your logic." This is a high-risk strategy since you might alienate him. Only experienced interviewers use it, and then only rarely.

Although the interview should feel like an unstructured conversation, it should clearly follow the path that you set out in the interview guide. Maintaining the right balance between your need to get your questions answered and the interviewee's need to get his point of view heard can be precarious. If you are not sensitive to the situation, guiding the interview may feel to the interviewee as though you are dominating it, probing can feel like cross-examination, a suggestion can feel like a demand, and drawing someone out may feel as though you are pumping him for information. Threatening questions should be made acceptable by building up to them through a logical line of conversation in nonthreatening areas.

The Way You Listen. Perhaps the most challenging aspect of interviewing is giving the interviewee a chance to talk. Typically, the smarter you are, the worse you listen, so you need to develop techniques to maintain your attention and manage your impatience.[2] First, you should develop the discipline of concentration. Pay close attention to what the interviewee is saying, and be sure that the questions you formulate fit with his comments, as well as your next line of questioning. You have to listen to be able to test your understanding and probe effectively.

Don't fill blank space. Silence burdens the interviewee to fill the pause. If you fill the space with comments and questions, the interviewee doesn't have to say anything. You may be able to encourage the interviewee to keep talking just by nodding your head, or saying innocuous phrases such as, "Really!" "Hmmmm . . . ," and "Uh-huh."

Listen to the interviewee's word choices. Reflect on the meaning and the feelings they indicate. Think about the implications of both. Concentrate on both verbal and nonverbal clues. The way the interviewee is sitting and the enthusiasm with which he gestures may give you insight into what he really feels. Remember that people always know what they think but not necessarily what they do. They will give you descriptions of how they think things are or how they would like them to be. They may not, and may not be able to, describe how things actually are and what they really do. It is up to you to listen and interpret what they say and how they behave. Most people are reticent to generate or express negative feelings, but they are much less able to suppress them physically.

Avoid the fast response. Be careful not to talk while the interviewee is talking, even if you are absolutely positive that you know what he is going to say next. Certainly, never try to help the interviewee along by finishing his sentences. You have to let him move at his own pace, regardless of how excruciatingly slow that might be.

Neutralize your feelings about what the interviewee says. If you react emotionally to his answers, you won't be able to understand them thoroughly. Do not respond when you disagree with the interviewee without first summarizing what he has said to his satisfaction. Be sure that you agree on what you disagree about. If you have strong preconceived notions about what the interviewee is talking about, you may not even hear what he says. It happens all the time.

When interviewing destitute men in New York in 1914, one interviewer found that 78 percent got there because of alcohol. Another claimed that the misfortunes of most of the men he interviewed were due to economic conditions. The first interviewer was a prohibitionist and the second was a socialist.[3] Remember that one person's terrorist is another's freedom fighter. Your job as an interviewer is to tease out what the interviewee perceives, not to support what you perceive.

An important part of listening is checking that you heard correctly. At appropriate points in the interview, such as the end of a series of questions about a particular topic, summarize what you have heard to make sure that you got it right. The summary will ensure both you and the interviewee that there is no misunderstanding between you.

The Way You Record the Data. Part of the challenge of any interview is recording what you learn. After all, the purpose of an interview is to capture data in sufficient detail to test your hypotheses or understand the situation. You want to be sure to record as much as possible, including the interviewee's phrasing and your perceptions of his body language, the office he's in, and so forth. However, you also want to keep the conversation going and not be hampered by your note taking.

While it may seem as though a tape recorder solves these problems, it has several shortcomings. It doesn't record expressions, it is boring to listen to after the fact, tapes are expensive and laborious to transcribe, and it may intimidate the interviewee.

Mike Hastings tells a story about his first and only experience with taping interviews. He had six interviews to conduct in a single day and decided to take along a tape recorder because he wouldn't have time between interviews to clean up his hand-written notes. He asked each of his interviewees if they would mind being recorded. No one objected, but three people asked him to turn off the recorder at some point during their discussions. As he tells it, "That's when the good stuff came out." At the end of the day, Mike went back to his car with a stack of tapes and thought he'd review the day on the long drive home. The drive was only two hours, and he had nearly nine hours worth of tapes, so he got nowhere.

Taking notes on paper is the most efficient way to collect the data. However, if there are two interviewers, do not fall into the trap of having one ask all the questions and the other take all the notes. The interviewee will wonder about the point of having the second interviewer in the room, the questioner may miss an important probe or question, and the note taker won't be able to record the questioner's perceptions. It is far better to have both interviewers take notes and record impressions. However, be sure to agree in advance which of you will take the lead in each part of the interview.

Always ask the interviewee for permission to take notes and explain the reason for them. If he objects, there is nothing you can do but acquiesce to his wishes.

To make the process easier, you may want to prepare your interview guide in such a way that you can capture your notes right on the guide. This enables you to structure your notes as you take them and also reminds you to stay on track. The only disadvantage is that if the interviewee takes you through the interview following a different path than you had planned on, a guide with lots of blank spaces may be harder to manage.

Ask the interviewee for copies of the materials that he refers to in the interview. Most will be happy to provide you with organization charts, process flow diagrams, operating statistics, and so forth.

Write the interview report as close to the end of the interview as possible. The half-life of conversations is very short. While most people find writing interview reports tedious, it is the only way to share interview data efficiently and effectively. The form that notes take doesn't matter too much, but consistency among project team members will make the write-ups more accessible.

The write-up should include the logistical details of the interview: who, when, where, contact information, and purpose. It should summarize the key findings of the interview and the implications of those findings. By capturing implications as you interview, you advance the thinking on your project. The write-up should record next steps and their deadlines. It should record your perceptions and observations and the other data you think should be collected or interviews that should be undertaken. Finally, it should record the details of the interview: what was said and in what manner. The details may prove to be useful as you summarize your findings to your client. Interview quotes have the potential to bring a set of conclusions to life. Figure B.2 provides a sample interview report.

Challenging Interviewees

Even when you prepare well, you will occasionally encounter someone who is difficult to interview. Be sensitive at the outset to the feelings and personality of the person you are talking with, and adjust your style to match his more closely if you can. Table B.3 provides suggestions about how you might handle challenging interviewees.

FIGURE B.2. SAMPLE INTERVIEW REPORT.

INTERVIEW NOTE

Interviewee Name and Title:

> Paul Bernard
> Vice President, New Product Development
> IJC Corporation

Contact Details:
> Room 613, Building C
> IJC Headquarters
> 22 Navigation Parkway
> Small City, OH
> Office: 440.221.3888
> Cell: 440.819.1313
> pmb@ijc.com

Purpose:
> Develop understanding of new product development role and position in organization

Date:
Location:
> October 19, 200X, 2:00–3:30 P.M.
> Dr. Bernard's office

Interviewer:
> Marianne Garms

Note preparer:
> Marianne Garms

Interview products
  ○ Tasks and responsibilities
  ○ New product development process
  ○ Department strengths and weaknesses

Next steps (action, responsibility, timing)

Perceptions, observations and implications

Interview details

TABLE B.3. INTERVIEWEE TYPES AND POSSIBLE RESPONSES TO THEM.

Type of Person	Possible Responses
Compulsive talker	Limit range of responses available. Avoid open questions as much as possible.
Nontalker	Figure out why if you can. Ask lots of open questions. Do not be afraid of silences.
Anxious interviewee	Provide a thorough orientation. Remain calm and relaxed. Avoid closed, rapid-fire questions. Provide lots of encouragement through body language and comments. Probe gently.

Angry or hostile interviewee	Be calm and interested.
	Listen for content, feelings, meanings.
	State your position, needs, feelings.
	Don't use "you" statements.
	Use "we" statements and provide lots of
	   rationale.
	Restate interviewee's opinion before
	   disagreeing with it.

Complainer	Don't agree or disagree; it will only offer encouragement. Paraphrase to show understanding.
Indecisive interviewee	Give time to provide responses. Offer to come back when he has thought through the data.
"Be nicers" afraid of causing conflict	Be very clear about the use of the information. Ensure him of your neutrality. Tell him he can't say anything that is wrong.
A "know-it-all"	Determine if the expertise is real or phony by asking for specifics as you probe.

Summary

Interviews are a key way to collect data for your project. The following list of do's and don'ts will help you conduct them effectively:

Do

- Prepare.
- Build rapport with the interviewee.

- Listen actively.
- Adjust your approach to the interviewee's behavior and reaction.
- Agree on next steps.
- Write comprehensive and thoughtful interview reports.

Don't

- Talk too much.
- Get distracted.
- Lead the interviewee.
- Make assumptions.
- Get into arguments.
- Make promises you can't keep.

NOTES

Introduction

1. S. Lohr, "He Loves to Win: At I.B.M., He Did," *New York Times,* Mar. 10, 2002, sec. 3, pp. 1, 11.

Chapter One

1. Often the word *transformation* is reserved for major changes to an organization, while *process* is used to describe ongoing activities. Here, I use *transformation* to mean either.
2. Checkland's work has influenced this chapter significantly. P. Checkland, *Systems Thinking, Systems Practice* (New York: John Wiley, 1981).
3. L. Gerstner, *Who Says Elephants Can't Dance?* (New York: Harper Collins, 2002).
4. Checkland, *Systems Thinking,* p. 317.

Chapter Two

1. This version of the story is the one I first heard. I later found out that Russell Ackoff tells a slight variation as well as many similar stories in his book, *The Art of Problem Solving* (New York: Wiley, 1978).
2. "Five whys" is described in P. Senge and others, *The Fifth Discipline Fieldbook* (New York: Doubleday, 1994).

Chapter Three

1. R. L. Daft and R. H. Lengel, "Organizational Information Requirements, Media Richness and Structural Design," *Management Science* 32:5 (1986): 554–571.

Chapter Four

1. D. K. Rigby, F. F. Reichheld, and P. Schefter, "Avoid the Four Perils of CRM," *Harvard Business Review* (Feb. 2002): 101–109.
2. I realize that *scoping* is not a word found in the dictionary. My PDN colleagues and I coined it several years ago when we were redesigning our approach to scope management. We prefer the gerund form to the noun *scope* as the former denotes the action inherent in the process and the diagram.
3. G. A. Miller, "The Magical Number Seven, Plus or Minus Two: Some Limits on Our Capacity for Processing Information," *Psychological Review* 63 (1956): 81–97.

Chapter Six

1. A PERT (Program Evaluation Review Technique) chart helps you schedule and coordinate tasks in a project. The process used is also known as the critical path method (CPM). A Gantt chart (so called because it was developed by Henry L. Gantt) is a graphical illustration of a project schedule. There are many excellent books and software programs that support both.

Chapter Seven

1. These keys to success are adapted from R. H. Schaffer, *High-Impact Consulting* (San Francisco: Jossey-Bass, 1997).
2. These filters have been adapted from E. Schein, *Process Consultation Revisited* (Reading, Mass.: Addison-Wesley, 1999).
3. The three ways people act are adapted from W. G. Bennis, K. D. Benne, and R. Chin (eds.), *The Planning of Change* (2nd ed.) (New York: Holt, 1969).

Chapter Eight

1. These labels and definitions come from V. Anderson and L. Hohnson, *System Thinking Basics* (Waltham, Mass.: Pegasus Communications, 1997).

Chapter Nine

1. The following example was taken from J. S. Dicey, *Fundamentals of Creative Thinking*, (San Francisco: New Lexington Press, 1989), p. 124.
2. J. Dewey, *How We Think* (Boston: Houghton Mifflin, 1910).
3. H. A. Simon, *The New Science of Management* (New York: HarperCollins, 1960).
4. A. L. Delbeq, A. H. VandeVen, and D. H. Gustafson, *Group Techniques for Program Planning: A Guide to Nominal Group and Delphi Processes* (Glencoe, Ill.: Scott, Foresman, 1975).
5. Plasticity and intrasensitivity are described in S. Plous, *The Psychology of Judgment and Decision Making* (New York: McGraw-Hill, 1993).

Chapter Ten

1. The following work influenced my thinking: B. Minto, *The Pyramid Principle* (London: Barbara Minto, 1996).
2. P. C. Neuhauser, *Corporate Legends and Lore* (Austin, Tex.: PCN Associates, 1993).
3. J. Martin and M. E. Powers, "Truth or Corporate Propaganda: The Value of a Good War Story," in L. R. Pondy, P. J. Frost, G. Morgan, and T. C. Dandridge (eds.), *Organization Symbolism* (Greenwich, Conn.: JAI Press, 1983).
4. I learned about the value of headlines while I was at McKinsey & Company. Gene Zelazny deserves the credit for this example.
5. K. Lewin, *Field Theory in Social Science* (New York: HarperCollins, 1951).

Appendix A

1. Available on-line: www.gowcb.com/products/systems/PDF/9628PROCESSEDCHEESE.PDF.
2. G. A. Rummler and A. P. Brache, *Improving Performance* (San Francisco: Jossey-Bass, 1995).

Appendix B

1. Argyris and Schön described valid and invalid inquiry types as Model 1 and Model 2. They first described the kinds of questions people ask when using each type in C. Argyris and D. Schön, *Organizational Learning: A Theory of Action Perspective* (Reading, Mass.: Addison-Wesley, 1978).
2. C. Argyris, "Teaching Smart People How to Learn," *Harvard Business Review*, May–June 1991, pp. 99–109.
3. S. Rice, "Contagious Bias in the Interview: A Methodological Note." *American Journal of Sociology* 35 (1929): 420–423.

INDEX

HOW TO USE THE CD-ROM

System Requirements

Windows PC

- 486 or Pentium processor-based personal computer
- Microsoft Windows 95 or Windows NT 3.51 or later
- Minimum RAM: 8 MB for Windows 95 and NT
- Available space on hard disk: 8 MB Windows 95 and NT
- 2X speed CD-ROM drive or faster
- Netscape 4.0 or higher browser or MS Internet Explorer 4.0 or higher
- Microsoft Word 97 or higher

Macintosh

- Macintosh with a 68020 or higher processor or Power Macintosh
- Apple OS version 7.0 or later
- Minimum RAM: 12 MB for Macintosh
- Available space on hard disk: 6 MB Macintosh
- 2X speed CD-ROM drive or faster
- Netscape 4.0 or higher browser or MS Internet Explorer 4.0 or higher
- Microsoft Word 98 or higher

NOTE: This CD also requires the free Acrobat Reader. You can download these products using the links below:
http://www.netscape.com/download/index.html
http://www.adobe.com/products/acrobat/readstep.html

Getting Started

Insert the CD-ROM into your drive. The CD-ROM will usually launch automatically. If it does not, click on the CD-ROM drive on your computer to launch. You will see an opening page. You can click on this page or wait for it to fade to the Copyright Page. After you click to agree to the terms of the Copyright Page, the Home Page will appear.

Moving Around

Use the buttons at the left of each screen or the text at the bottom of each screen to move among the menu pages. To view a document listed on one of the menu pages, simply click on the name of the document. Use the scrollbar at the right of the screen to scroll up and down each page. To quit a document at any time, click the box at the upper right-hand corner of the screen.

To quit the CD-ROM, you can click the Quit button on the left of each menu page or hit Control-Q if you are a PC user or Command-Q if you are a Mac user.

In Case of Trouble

If you experience difficulty using this CD-ROM, please follow these steps:

1. Make sure your hardware and systems configurations conform to the systems requirements noted under "Systems Requirements" above.
2. Review the installation procedure for your type of hardware and operating system. It is possible to reinstall the software if necessary.
3. You may call Jossey-Bass Customer Care at (800) 274-4434 between the hours of 8 A.M. and 4 P.M. Eastern Standard Time, and ask for Jossey-Bass Product Support. It is also possible to contact Product Support by e-mail at *techsupport@JosseyBass.com.*

Please have the following information available:

- Type of computer and operating system
- Version of Windows or Mac OS being used
- Any error messages displayed
- Complete description of the problem

(It is best if you are sitting at your computer when making the call.)